First World War

and Army of Occupation

War Diary

France, Belgium and Germany

59 DIVISION
178 Infantry Brigade
Sherwood Foresters
(Nottinghamshire and Derbyshire Regiment)
2/5th Battalion
16 October 1914 - 3 August 1918

WO95/3025/1

The Naval & Military Press Ltd
www.nmarchive.com
Published in association with The National Archives

Published by

The Naval & Military Press Ltd

Unit 10 Ridgewood Industrial Park,

Uckfield, East Sussex,

TN22 5QE England

Tel: +44 (0) 1825 749494

www.naval-military-press.com

www.nmarchive.com

Contents

Document type	Place/Title	Date From	Date To
Heading	WO 3025 59th Div 178 Bde 2/5 Bn Sherwood Foresters 1914-Oct-1916 Feb		
Heading	59 Div 178 Bde 2/5 Bn. Sherwood Foresters 1914 Oct-1916 Feb.		
Heading	War Diary Of 2/5th Sherwood Foresters. October To December 1914.		
Miscellaneous	Officer Commanding	25/10/1915	25/10/1915
War Diary	Derby	16/10/1914	21/11/1914
War Diary	Swanwich	01/12/1914	31/12/1914
Heading	War Diaries Of 2/5th Sherwood Foresters January To December 1915		
War Diary	Swanwich	01/01/1915	31/01/1915
War Diary	Swanwick	01/02/1915	02/02/1915
War Diary	Luton	03/02/1915	04/06/1915
War Diary	Dunstable	11/06/1915	09/08/1915
War Diary	Watford	31/08/1915	30/09/1915
Miscellaneous	Statement To Accompany War Diary, For The Month Of September, 1915.		
War Diary	Walford (Camp)	01/10/1915	31/10/1915
Miscellaneous	Statement To Accompany The War Diary For The Month Of October 1915.		
War Diary	Watford	01/11/1915	30/11/1915
Miscellaneous	2/5th. Battalion. The Sherwood Foresters.	07/12/1915	07/12/1915
Miscellaneous	2/5th Bn. Sherwood Foresters.		
War Diary	Watford	01/12/1915	31/12/1915
Miscellaneous	2/5th. Battalion, The Sherwood Foresters.	07/01/1916	07/01/1916
Miscellaneous	178th. Infantry Brigade. Watford.	15/12/1915	15/12/1915
Heading	War Diary Of 2/5th Batt. Sherwood Foresters From 1st To 31st January 1916 Volume XV		
War Diary	Watford	06/01/1916	31/01/1916
Miscellaneous	2/5th. Battalion. The Sherwood Foresters.	05/02/1916	05/02/1916
Heading	War Diary Of 2/5th Batt. Sherwood Foresters.		
War Diary	Watford	02/02/1916	29/02/1916
Miscellaneous	2/5 The Battalion, Sherwood Foresters.	07/03/1916	07/03/1916
Heading	WO 3025 59th Div 2-5th Bn Notts & Durby Regt 1917-Feb-1918 July.		
Heading	59th Division 178th Infy Bde 2-5th Bn Notts & Derby Regt Feb 1917-Jly 1919		
War Diary	Hurdcott	23/02/1917	25/02/1917
War Diary	Folkestone Boulogne	26/02/1917	26/02/1917
War Diary	Vers	27/02/1917	27/02/1917
War Diary	St Fucien	28/02/1917	28/03/1917
War Diary	Flechin Vendelles	03/04/1917	10/04/1917
War Diary	Hervilly	18/04/1917	28/04/1917
Miscellaneous	2/5th. Battalion, Notts & Derby Regiment.		
War Diary		01/05/1917	31/05/1917
Operation(al) Order(s)	Operation Orders No. 2. by Major R.B. Rickman Commanding 2/5th Battalion Notts & Derby Regiment	02/05/1917	02/05/1917
Miscellaneous	Addendum No.1 To 2/5th. Operation Order No. 2		
Map	Map		

War Diary	Metz En-Couture France	01/06/1917	05/06/1917
War Diary	Equancourt	11/06/1917	12/06/1917
War Diary	Dessart Wood (W.I.)	21/06/1917	30/06/1917
War Diary	Villers Plouich	01/07/1917	09/07/1917
War Diary	0.35 (Sheet 57c SE)	09/07/1917	28/07/1917
War Diary	Le Mesnil En Arrouaise France Sheet 57c 0.35d.	01/08/1917	24/08/1917
War Diary	Bruce Huts Aveluy (Albert Ambinous Sheet 1/40000) W.16a	24/08/1917	31/08/1917
War Diary	France Ref. Map. Sheet 27. J.2.a 80.	31/08/1917	20/09/1917
War Diary	France Ref. Map Sheet 27. L.8c.35	21/09/1917	23/09/1917
War Diary	Sheet 28 NW Belgium G 6 D 4 4.	24/09/1917	30/09/1917
Map	Map		
Miscellaneous	Message Form.		
Operation(al) Order(s)	Operation Order No. 22 by Lieut Col H.R. Gadd M.C. Commanding 2/5th Sherwood Foresters	24/09/1917	24/09/1917
Operation(al) Order(s)	Operation Order No. 21 by Lieut Col H.R. Gadd M.C. Commanding 2/5th Sherwood Foresters	25/09/1917	25/09/1917
Miscellaneous	2/5th Battalion The Sherwood Foresters.	26/09/1917	26/09/1917
Operation(al) Order(s)	Operation Order No. 23 by Lieut Col H.R. Gadd M.C. Commanding 2/5th Sherwood Foresters	29/09/1917	29/09/1917
War Diary	Les Ciseaux	01/10/1917	05/10/1917
War Diary	Delette	06/10/1917	13/10/1917
War Diary	Gouy Servins	14/10/1917	31/10/1917
Operation(al) Order(s)	Operation Orders No. 24 by Lt Col H.R. Gadd Commanding 2/5th Battalion The Sherwood Foresters	01/10/1917	01/10/1917
Operation(al) Order(s)	Operation Order No. 25 by Lieut Colonel H.R. Gadd M.C. Commanding 2/5th Sherwood Foresters	04/10/1917	04/10/1917
Operation(al) Order(s)	Operation Order No. 27 By Major C.R.C. Trench Commanding 2/5th Battalion The Sherwood Foresters	10/10/1917	10/10/1917
Operation(al) Order(s)	Operation Orders No. 29 By Major C.R.C. Trench Commanding 2/5th Battalion The Sherwood Foresters		
Operation(al) Order(s)	Operation Order No. 30 By Major C.R.C Trench Commanding 2/5th Battalion The Sherwood Foresters	12/10/1917	12/10/1917
Operation(al) Order(s)	Operation Order By Major C.R.C. Trench Commanding 2/5th Battalion The Sherwood Foresters	20/10/1917	20/10/1917
Operation(al) Order(s)	Order No. 36. by Lieut Colonel H.R. Gadd M.C. Commanding 2/5th Battalion Sherwood Foresters	26/10/1917	26/10/1917
Operation(al) Order(s)	Appendix to Operation Orders No.32	28/10/1917	28/10/1917
Miscellaneous	Operation Orders No. 32 by Lieut Colonel H.R. M.C. Gadd Commanding 2/5th Battalion The Sherwood Foresters	29/10/1917	29/10/1917
War Diary	Noue	01/11/1917	09/11/1917
War Diary	Souchez Nove	10/11/1917	23/11/1917
War Diary	Equancourt	24/11/1917	26/11/1917
War Diary	Marcoing	27/11/1917	27/11/1917
War Diary	Equancourt	28/11/1917	28/11/1917
War Diary	Trescault	29/11/1917	30/11/1917
War Diary	Trescault	01/12/1917	07/12/1917
War Diary	Flesquires	08/12/1917	09/12/1917
War Diary	Ribecourt	10/12/1917	20/12/1917
War Diary	Barastre	21/12/1917	23/12/1917
War Diary	Beavlencourt	24/12/1917	25/12/1917
War Diary	Houvin Houvigneul	26/12/1917	31/12/1917
Operation(al) Order(s)	Operation Orders No 41. by Lieut Colonel H.R. Gadd M.C. Commanding 2/5th Battalion Sherwood Foresters	03/12/1917	03/12/1917

Operation(al) Order(s)	Operation Order No 42. by Lieut Colonel H.R. Gadd M.C. Commanding 2/5th Battalion Sherwood Foresters	04/12/1917	04/12/1917
Miscellaneous		09/12/1917	09/12/1917
Operation(al) Order(s)	Operation Order No 48 by Lt Col H.R. Gadd M.C.	10/12/1917	10/12/1917
Operation(al) Order(s)	Operation Order No 49 by Lt Colonel H.R. Gadd M.C. Commanding 2/5th Battalion Sherwood Foresters	15/12/1917	15/12/1917
Operation(al) Order(s)	Operation Orders No.50 by Lt Colonel H.R. Gadd M.C. Commanding 2/5th Battalion Sherwood Foresters	15/12/1917	15/12/1917
Operation(al) Order(s)	Operation Order No. 51 by Lt Colonel H.R. Gadd M.C. Commanding 2/5th Battalion Sherwood Foresters	17/12/1917	17/12/1917
Operation(al) Order(s)	Operation Orders No 51 by Lt Colonel H.R. Gadd M.C. Commanding 2/5th Battalion Sherwood Foresters	18/12/1917	18/12/1917
Operation(al) Order(s)	Operation Order No 52 by Lt Colonel H.R. Gadd M.C. Commanding 2/5th Battalion Sherwood Foresters	20/12/1917	20/12/1917
Operation(al) Order(s)	Operation Orders No 53 by Lt Colonel H.R. Gadd M.C. Commanding 2/5th Battalion The Sherwood Foresters	22/12/1917	22/12/1917
Operation(al) Order(s)	Operation Orders No 54 by Lt Colonel H.R. Gadd M.C. Commanding 2/5th Battalion The Sherwood Foresters	23/12/1917	23/12/1917
Miscellaneous	Operation Order No.54 By Lieut Colonel H.R Gadd M.C. Commanding 2/5th Battalion The Sherwood Foresters	24/12/1917	24/12/1917
War Diary	Houvin Houvigneul	01/01/1918	08/02/1918
War Diary	Bavincourt	09/02/1918	09/02/1918
War Diary	Boisleux Marc	10/02/1918	10/02/1918
War Diary	Mory	11/02/1918	28/02/1918
Operation(al) Order(s)	Operation Orders No. 56 by Lt Colonel H.R. Gadd M.C. Commanding 2/5th Battalion The Sherwood Foresters	05/02/1918	05/02/1918
Operation(al) Order(s)	Operation Orders No.57 by Lt Colonel H.R. Gadd M.C. Commanding 2/5th Battalion Sherwood Foresters	07/02/1918	07/02/1918
Operation(al) Order(s)	Operation Orders No.58 by Lt Colonel H.R. Gadd M.C. Commanding 2/5th Battalion The Sherwood Foresters	08/02/1918	08/02/1918
Miscellaneous	Operation Orders No 58. by Lieut Colonel H.R. Gadd M.C. Commanding 2/5th Battalion The Sherwood Foresters	08/02/1918	08/02/1918
Operation(al) Order(s)	Operation Orders No. 59 by Lieut Colonel H.R. Gadd M.C. Commanding 2/5th Battalion The Sherwood Foresters	09/02/1918	09/02/1918
Operation(al) Order(s)	Operation Orders No.56 by Lieut Colonel H.R. Gadd M.C. Commanding 2/5th Battalion The Sherwood Foresters	10/02/1918	10/02/1918
Operation(al) Order(s)	Operation Orders No.60 by Lieut Colonel H.R. Gadd M.C. Commanding 2/5th Battalion Sherwood Foresters	13/02/1918	13/02/1918
Operation(al) Order(s)	R.A.M.C. Orders No.61		
Miscellaneous	2/5th. Battalion, The Sherwood Foresters.		
Operation(al) Order(s)	Operation Order No 62 by Lt Colonel H.R. Gadd M.C. Commanding 2/5th Battalion Sherwood Foresters	16/02/1918	16/02/1918
Operation(al) Order(s)	Operation Order No. 63 by Major C.R.E. Trench Commanding 2/5th Bn Sherwood Foresters	22/02/1918	22/02/1918
Operation(al) Order(s)	Operation Order No. 65 by Major C.R.E. Trench Commanding 2/5th Battalion Sherwood Foresters	22/02/1918	22/02/1918
Miscellaneous	Operation Orders No.65 by Major C.R.E. Trench Commanding 2/5th Battalion The Sherwood Foresters	22/02/1918	22/02/1918
Operation(al) Order(s)	Orders No.1. By Major G.R.C.Trench. Commanding 2/5th Battn Sherwood Foresters		
Heading	59th Division.176th Infantry Brigade.		

War Diary	S Of Caoisilles	02/03/1918	02/03/1918
War Diary	Mory	02/03/1918	02/03/1918
War Diary	Noreuil	10/03/1918	21/03/1918
War Diary	Ervillers	21/03/1918	22/03/1918
War Diary	Senlis	23/03/1918	25/03/1918
War Diary	Bavelin Court	26/03/1918	26/03/1918
War Diary	Fieffes	28/03/1918	28/03/1918
War Diary	Cambligneul	30/03/1918	30/03/1918
Miscellaneous	2/5th Batt. Sherwood Foresters.		
Operation(al) Order(s)	Operation Order No. 64 by Major C.R. Chenevix Trench Commanding. 2/5th Bn The Sherwood Foresters	01/03/1918	01/03/1918
Miscellaneous	Operation Order 64 by Major C.R. Chenevix Trench Commanding. 2/5th Bn The Sherwood Foresters	01/03/1918	01/03/1918
Miscellaneous	Orders By Major C.E Division Trench.	05/03/1918	05/03/1918
Operation(al) Order(s)	Operation Order No. 65 by Lt Colonel H.R. Gadd M.C. Commanding 2/5th Battalion Sherwood Foresters	09/03/1918	09/03/1918
Miscellaneous	Operation Orders No.65 by Lieut Colonel H.R. Gadd M.C. Commanding 2/5th Battalion The Sherwood Foresters	09/03/1918	09/03/1918
Miscellaneous	2/5th. Battalion, The Sherwood Foresters.		
Miscellaneous	2/5th Batt. The Sherwood Foresters	14/05/1918	14/05/1918
Operation(al) Order(s)	Order No. 69 by Lieut Colonel H.R. Gadd M.C. Commanding 2/5th Battalion Sherwood Foresters	19/03/1918	19/03/1918
Operation(al) Order(s)	Order No. 65 by Lieut Colonel H.R. Gadd M.C. Commanding 2/5th Battalion Sherwood Foresters		
Miscellaneous	Copy Of Letter From Br. General. T.W. Stansfield. CMG. DSO.		
Heading	178th Brigade. 59th Division. 2/5th Battalion April 1918.		
War Diary	Cambligneul	01/04/1918	01/04/1918
War Diary	St Jan-Ter Biezen	02/04/1918	07/04/1918
War Diary	Winnezeele Area	08/04/1918	10/04/1918
War Diary	Brandhoek Area	11/04/1918	12/04/1918
War Diary	Kemmel	13/04/1918	13/04/1918
War Diary	(HQ In Railway)	13/04/1918	14/04/1918
War Diary	(HQ N326 79)	14/04/1918	15/04/1918
War Diary	Kemmel	15/04/1918	19/04/1918
War Diary	Westoutre	20/04/1918	20/04/1918
War Diary	Brandhoek Area	21/04/1918	26/04/1918
War Diary	St Jan Ter Biezen	27/04/1918	29/04/1918
War Diary	Houtkerque	30/04/1918	30/04/1918
Operation(al) Order(s)	Operation Orders No. 1 by Major R.S. Pratt M.C. Commanding 2/5th Battalion The Sherwood Foresters	06/08/1918	06/08/1918
Miscellaneous	2/5th Battalion The Sherwood Foresters		
Operation(al) Order(s)	Operation Order No. 2 by Lt Col A.C. Baines Comdg 2/5 Bn Sherwood Foresters	28/04/1918	28/04/1918
War Diary	Houtkerque	01/05/1918	05/05/1918
War Diary	St Omer	06/05/1918	09/05/1918
War Diary	Blessy	10/05/1918	10/05/1918
War Diary	Bours	11/05/1918	30/05/1918
Operation(al) Order(s)	2/5th. Battalion, The Sherwood Foresters Order No. 3	01/05/1918	01/05/1918
Miscellaneous	2/5th. Battalion, The Sherwood Foresters Order No. 4	06/05/1918	06/05/1918
Miscellaneous	2/5th. Battalion, The Sherwood Foresters Order No. 4	08/05/1918	08/05/1918
Operation(al) Order(s)	2/5th. Battalion, Sherwood Foresters Order No. 5	09/05/1918	09/05/1918
War Diary	Bours	01/06/1918	02/06/1918
War Diary	Preures	03/06/1918	11/06/1918

War Diary	Bezinghem	12/06/1918	30/06/1918
Operation(al) Order(s)	2/5th. Battalion, The Sherwood Foresters Order No. 4	01/06/1918	01/06/1918
Operation(al) Order(s)	2/5th. Battalion. The Sherwood Foresters Order No. 2		
Operation(al) Order(s)	2/5th. Battalion, The Sherwood Foresters Order No. 7		
Operation(al) Order(s)	2/5th, Battalion, Sherwood Foresters Order No. 8	02/06/1918	02/06/1918
War Diary	Bezinghem	01/07/1918	03/08/1918
Operation(al) Order(s)	2/5th. Battalion, The Sherwood Foresters Order No. 9		

WO 3025 59th DIV

178 Bde

2/5 BN SHERWOOD FORESTERS

1914 - Oct - 1916 FEB

59 DIV

178 BDE

2/5 BN. SHERWOOD FORESTERS

1914 OCT — 1916 FEB

War Diaries of
2/5th Sherwood Foresters.

October & December
1914.

Confidential

War Diary

of

Headquarters ~~2/1 Sherwood Foresters Infantry Brigade~~

from ~~1–30 April 1915~~

~~Volume III~~

178/9/5.

From:- Officer Commanding

2/5th Battalion, The Sherwood Foresters

To:- Headquarters

178th Infantry Brigade

Watford.

WAR DIARY

In accordance with your letter 1271/29 dated 15/10/15.

I herewith enclose War Diary for October and November 1914 - December 1914, and September 1915.

Battalion Orders at commencement were only issued weekly, and consisted in most cases simply of postings to Companies.

Very little information is obtainable, as to the early ~~working~~ history of the Battalion.

G. C. Aitchison

Lieut-Colonel,
Cmm'g 2/5th Battalion, The Sherwood Foresters.

Watford
25/10/15.

Confidential

2/5th Bn Sherwood Foresters

Army Form C. 2118.

Instructions regarding War Diaries and Intelligence Summaries are contained in F. S. Regs., Part II. and the Staff Manual respectively. Title pages will be prepared in manuscript.

WAR DIARY
or
INTELLIGENCE SUMMARY.
(Erase heading not required.)

Place	Date 1914	Hour	Summary of Events and Information	Remarks and references to Appendices
Derby	October		The first men were enlisted under date 5/10/14 at the following places:- Derby, Belper, Swadlincote Long Eaton, Ilkeston. 70 men were attested and promotions of old N.C.Os were made.	
	16th		First Battalion Orders issued by Lieut: Col. Maurice Hunter T.D. under heading of 5th (Home Service) Batt. Notts + Derby Regt. These orders were signed W R.H. Whiston, Major + acting Adjutant. Certain men were posted to Companies + first promotions to N.C.O's were made.	
	23rd		Battalion Orders No 2 were issued under heading 5th Reserve Battalion, Notts + Derby Regt. 192 men were attested + posted to Companies	
			General.	
	24th		An advance party went to Swanwick (The Hayes) As further men were enlisted and clothed they were sent forward to The Hayes, Swanwick, to join the Regiment.	
	30th		Battalion Orders No 3 of this date shewed 309 men attested and posted to Companies. The same date 38 men were transferred to No 4 Section North Mid. Divisional Ammn. Column. 571 men were enlisted during the month	
	November 7th		No. 4 Battalion Orders. Sergt Instr. Poole was posted to this Batt. 219 men were enlisted + posted to Companies. 6 men were transferred to the 1/5th and taken on the strength. 2 men were struck off the strength as Medically unfit.	
	14th		Battalion orders No 5 dated 14th November '14 give extracts from Gazette of 2nd November shewing appointment of Lieut. Colonel M. Hunter from Territorial Force Reserve to be Lieut. Col. (Temporary). Dated 18th September '14.	

2353 Wt. W2544/1454 700,000 5/15 D. D. & L. A.D.S.S./Forms/C. 2118.

Instructions regarding War Diaries and Intelligence Summaries are contained in F. S. Regs., Part II. and the Staff Manual respectively. Title pages will be prepared in manuscript.

WAR DIARY
or
INTELLIGENCE SUMMARY.
(Erase heading not required.)

Army Form C. 2118.

Place	Date	Hour	Summary of Events and Information	Remarks and references to Appendices
	1914			
Derby	November 14th		Tom Matthewson Woodward (Late Colour Sergt + Acting Sergt Major) to be Quartermaster with honorary rank of Lieut., dated 2nd October '14.	
			From the Gazette of 5th November 1914.	
			Capt. + Hon. Major John Robert Pinder (retired list) to be Major (Temporary) dated 1st October '14	
			The undermentioned to be Captains (Temporary) dated 1st October '14.	
			John Theodore Wykes (late Capt. 1st Vol. Batt. Notts + Derby Regt)	
			Gerard Gibson Baily (late Capt. 5th Sherwood Foresters)	
			Frederick Edward Mowbray Sonne (late Capt. 5th Sherwood Foresters)	
			Horace Montague Clifford (late Capt. 1st Vol. Batt. Notts + Derby Regt)	
			Alfred Henry Longden (late Capt. 5th Sherwood Foresters)	
			Extract from Gazette, dated 9th November 1914.	
			Capt. Bertram J.S. Crossley resigns his Commission on account of ill health dated 10th Nov. 1914.	
			224 men were enlisted. A draft of 130 men were transferred to the 1/5th Batt. and struck off the strength. 4 men were discharged. 3 as medically unfit and 1 as "unsatisfactory conduct"	
	21st		About the 15th or 16th Nov. recruiting was stopped	
			By the end of the month the whole of the Battalion were in training at Swanwick.	
			At the end of the month the strength of the Battalion was 882 NCOs + men	

2353 Wt. W2544/1454 700,000 5/15 D. D. & L. A.D.S.S./Forms/C. 2118.

Instructions regarding War Diaries and Intelligence Summaries are contained in F. S. Regs., Part II. and the Staff Manual respectively. Title pages will be prepared in manuscript.

WAR DIARY
or
INTELLIGENCE SUMMARY.
(Erase heading not required.)

Army Form C. 2118.

2/5 Nr Sherwood Forester

Place	Date	Hour	Summary of Events and Information	Remarks and references to Appendices
Swanwich	1914 December 1st		The Battalion paraded for general training. 9 men were taken on the strength from the 1st/5th Batt. 2 men were discharged as medically unfit. M. J. Hunter gazetted as 2nd Lieut with effect from this date.	
	2		The Battalion orders No 8 were on this date issued at Swanwich.	
	2nd	do	The Battalion paraded for route march	
	3rd	do	The Battalion paraded & carried out general training. 10 men were transferred to the 1/5th Batt	

Instructions regarding War Diaries and Intelligence Summaries are contained in F. S. Regs., Part II. and the Staff Manual respectively. Title pages will be prepared in manuscript.

WAR DIARY

~~INTELLIGENCE SUMMARY~~.

(Erase heading not required.)

Army Form C. 2118.

Place	Date 1914.	Hour	Summary of Events and Information	Remarks and references to Appendices
Swanwick	December 4th		The Battalion paraded for general training. Pay. A kit inspection was held.	
	5th	do	The Battalion paraded for general training. E F Ann was gazetted as a 2nd Lieut on this date.	
	6th		The Battalion paraded for Divine Service.	

2353 Wt. W2544/1454 700,000 5/15 D. D. & L. A.D.S.S./Forms/C. 2118.

Army Form C. 2118.

WAR DIARY

~~or~~

~~INTELLIGENCE SUMMARY~~.

(*Erase heading not required.*)

Instructions regarding War Diaries and Intelligence Summaries are contained in F. S. Regs., Part II. and the Staff Manual respectively. Title pages will be prepared in manuscript.

Place	Date 1914	Hour	Summary of Events and Information	Remarks and references to Appendices
Swanwich	December 7th		The Battalion paraded for general training. A & B Companies carried out Musketry practice. "C" & "D" Companies had Lectures.	
	8th	do	The Battalion paraded for general training. C & D Companies carried out Musketry practice.	
	9th	do	The Battalion paraded for general training. F & G Companies entertained visitors. E & F. Companies carried out Musketry Practice.	

2353 Wt. W2544/1454 700,000 5/15 D. D. & L. A.D.S.S./Forms/C. 2118.

Instructions regarding War Diaries and Intelligence Summaries are contained in F. S. Regs., Part II. and the Staff Manual respectively. Title pages will be prepared in manuscript.

WAR DIARY

~~or~~

~~INTELLIGENCE SUMMARY~~.

(Erase heading not required.)

Army Form C. 2118.

Place	Date 1914	Hour	Summary of Events and Information	Remarks and references to Appendices
Woolwich	December 10th		Extract from Gazette of the 4th December 1914 Private Edwin Francis Ann from 4th Public Schools Battalion Royal Fusiliers to be Second Lieutenant dated 5th Dec '14	
	15th		The Commanding Officer held an Examination of all N. C. O's in Squad Section Company Drill & Rifle Exercises 3 men transferred to the 1/5th Battalion. 2 men were transferred from the 1/5th Batt.	
	16th		10 men were transferred to the 1/5th Battalion & 1 man was transferred from the 1/5th Battalion.	

2353 Wt. W2514/1454 700,000 5/15 D. D. & L. A.D.S.S./Forms/C. 2118.

Instructions regarding War Diaries and Intelligence Summaries are contained in F. S. Regs., Part II. and the Staff Manual respectively. Title pages will be prepared in manuscript.

WAR DIARY

~~or~~

~~INTELLIGENCE SUMMARY.~~

(Erase heading not required.)

Army Form C. 2118.

Place	Date 1914	Hour	Summary of Events and Information	Remarks and references to Appendices
Swanwich	December 17th		A & B Company N. C. O's paraded for Examination. Extract from Gazette of 10th Dec '14. Geoffrey Nutt to be 2nd Lieut dated 28th November 1914	
	22nd	do	3 men transferred from the 1/5th Battalion.	
	23		B & C Companies entertained visitors. 1 man was transferred from the South Wales Hussars	

2353 Wt. W2544/1454 700,000 5/15 D. D. & L. A.D.S.S./Forms/C. 2118.

Instructions regarding War Diaries and Intelligence Summaries are contained in F. S. Regs., Part II. and the Staff Manual respectively. Title pages will be prepared in manuscript.

WAR DIARY

~~INTELLIGENCE SUMMARY~~.

(Erase heading not required.)

Army Form C. 2118.

Place	Date 1914	Hour	Summary of Events and Information	Remarks and references to Appendices
Swanwich	December 24th		Extracts from Gazette of 16th December 1914 Maurice Ford Hunter to be 2nd Lieut dated 1st December 1914 Private Harry Dennis Melville Wright to be 2nd Lieut dated 18th Dec '14	
	29th		There were no orders issued between these dates	
	30th		7 men were taken on the strength from the 1/5th Batt	
	31st		1 man was struck off the strength for unsatisfactory conduct	

2353 Wt. W2544/1454 700,000 5/15 D. D. & L. A.D.S.S./Forms/C. 2118.

War Diaries of

2/5th Sherwood Foresters.

January to December
191~~4~~5.

143 Bde

Misc

Apl 1917

May

Volume No. ....

BRITISH SALONIKA FORCE

WAR DIARY.

28th DIVISION

Vol. No.	Unit	PERIOD From	PERIOD To
29	Commanding Royal Artillery	1/3/18	31/3/18
30	3rd Brigade R. F. A.,	do	do
28	31st do	do	do
26	130th do	do	do
34	54th do	do	do

A.P. & S.D., Alex./No. 752/8:5:17/3000 (5004IG/53) W. M. & Co.

Confidential

9/5th Bn S7

Army Form C. 2118.

WAR DIARY
or
~~INTELLIGENCE SUMMARY.~~
(Erase heading not required.)

Instructions regarding War Diaries and Intelligence Summaries are contained in F. S. Regs., Part II. and the Staff Manual respectively. Title pages will be prepared in manuscript.

Place	Date 1915	Hour	Summary of Events and Information	Remarks and references to Appendices
Bramwich	January 1st to 7th		The General training of the Battalion was carried out on these dates. Two men were discharged on the 5th inst for "unsatisfactory conduct". 22 men were taken on the strength on first enlistment on the 6th inst.	
	8th 9th		Nothing of importance occurred.	
	10th		50 N.C.O's men fired a course of Musketry on the Ripley miniature Range. Two men were discharged as "Medically unfit"	
	11th to 14th		The Battalion carried out general training on these dates.	
	15th		Four men were struck off the strength as no longer fit for War Service.	
	16th		Frank Woolley Smith (late cadet Wellingborough School Contingent Junior Division) to be 2nd Lieut dated 23rd December 1914. Two men were taken on the strength from the 1/5th Batt	
	18th		20 men were transferred to the 1/5th Battalion.	
	19th to 29th		Nothing of importance to record. General training was carried out	

2353 Wt. W2544/1454 700,000 5/15 D. D. & L. A.D.S.S./Forms/C. 2118.

Instructions regarding War Diaries and Intelligence Summaries are contained in F. S. Regs., Part II. and the Staff Manual respectively. Title pages will be prepared in manuscript.

WAR DIARY

~~or~~

~~INTELLIGENCE SUMMARY.~~

(Erase heading not required.)

Army Form C. 2118.

Place	Date	Hour	Summary of Events and Information	Remarks and references to Appendices
Swanwick	1915 January 30th		Orders having been received to form the Battalion under the double company establishment the following companies were formed together NO 1 Coy "B" & "E" NO 2 Coy "A" & "F" NO 3 Coy "D" & "H" NO 4 Coy "C" & "G"	
	31st		Nil	

[illegible]

2353 Wt. W2544/1454 700,000 5/15 D. D. & L. A.D.S.S./Forms/C. 2118

Confidential

Instructions regarding War Diaries and Intelligence Summaries are contained in F. S. Regs., Part II. and the Staff Manual respectively. Title Pages will be prepared in manuscript.

WAR DIARY
or
~~INTELLIGENCE SUMMARY~~
(Erase heading not required.)

Army Form C. 2118

2/5th Sherwood Foresters

Place	Date	Hour	Summary of Events and Information	Remarks and references to Appendices
	February 1915			
SWANWICK	1 & 2		Nothing of importance	
LUTON	3		The Bn moved from Swanwick to Luton being billeted there without Subsistence	
	4		Extract from London Gazette 5th Batt Notts & Derby Regt. George H Williamson to be 2nd Lt dated 22/1/15	
	5. 6 & 7		Nothing of importance	
	8		The Bn moved from Luton to Broxbourne & Hoddesdon being billeted there without Subsistence	
	9		48 men transferred to 1/5th Bn & struck off Strength 45 men transferred from 1/5th Bn & taken on Strength	
	10 to 21		Nothing of importance	
	22		2 NCOs & 23 men transferred to 1/5th Bn & struck off Strength	
	23		2nd Lt E. A. Crossley transferred to 1/5th Bn & struck off Strength 2 NCOs & 21 men transferred from 1/5th Bn & taken on Strength	
	24		The Bn moved to Luton being billeted there without Subsistence During the fortnight spent at Broxbourne & Hoddesdon the Bn was engaged in instruction in entrenching	
	25		4 NCOs & 25 men transferred from 1/5th Batt & taken on Strength	
	26		All NCOs & men of "K" Company (total 129) transferred to Companies 963 Rifles Japanese received & ammunition	

Confidential

Instructions regarding War Diaries and Intelligence Summaries are contained in F. S. Regs., Part II. and the Staff Manual respectively. Title Pages will be prepared in manuscript.

WAR DIARY
or
~~INTELLIGENCE SUMMARY~~
(Erase heading not required.)

Army Form C. 2118

2/5th Sherwood Foresters

Place	Date 1915	Hour	Summary of Events and Information	Remarks and references to Appendices
LUTON	March 1		100 recruits transferred from the Depôt & taken on Strength	
	2		Inspection by General Sir Ian Hamilton G.O.C in Chief	
	3 to 7		Nothing of Importance.	
	8		Japanese Musketry Course commenced today	
	9 to 11		Nothing of Importance	
	12		Musketry Course for Imp Service men with L E rifle commenced today	
	13 to 15		Nothing of Importance	
	16		Extract from London Gazette 5th Batt Sherwood Foresters William Beaumont Allwan to be 2nd Lt dated 11/3/15 15 men transferred to 1st reinforcement 1/5th Batt & struck off strength.	
	17 + 18		Nothing of importance	
	19		Extract from London Gazette. 5th Batt Sherwood Foresters Francis Herbert Sutherland to be 2nd Lt dated 26/2/15	
	20 to 23		Nothing of importance	
	24		Extract from London Gazette 5th Batt Sherwood Foresters Cadet Henry Drummond Hancock Oxford Univ O.T.C to be 2nd Lt dated 21/3/15 Major W.R.H Whiston & Capt H.M. Clifford posted to 3/5th Battn. Inoculation commenced	
	25		Extract from London Gazette 5th Batt Sherwood Foresters. Pte Frank Litherland Bailey from 6th Batt Royal Sussex Regt to be 2nd Lt dated 24/3/15 Pte Harold Shafto Danton from 5th (City of London) Batt The London Regt (Rifle Brigade) to be 2nd Lt dated 24/3/15. Imperial Service Company formed.	
	26 to 30.		Nothing of importance	
	31		34 L.D 12 R. + 9 P.C's received between 19/3/15 + this date + billeted in stables	

1875 Wt. W593/826 1,000,000 4/15 J.B.C. & A. A.D.S.S./Forms/C. 2118.

Confidential

Instructions regarding War Diaries and Intelligence Summaries are contained in F. S. Regs., Part II. and the Staff Manual respectively. Title Pages will be prepared in manuscript.

WAR DIARY
or
~~INTELLIGENCE SUMMARY~~
(Erase heading not required.)

Army Form C. 2118

2/5th Sherwood Foresters

Place	Date 1915	Hour	Summary of Events and Information	Remarks and references to Appendices
	April 1 to 11		Nothing of importance	
	12		Extract from London Gazette 5th Batt Sherwood Foresters Lt R B Rickman to be Capt (Temporary) dated 1.12.14 Lt P.B. Coles " " 1.12.14	
	13 to 14		Nothing of importance	
	15		3 N.C.O's + 98 men transferred to 3/5th Batt + struck off strength but remain attached to "C" company for Discipline Rations + Billets	
	16		Nothing of importance	
	17		Extract from London Gazette 5th Batt Sherwood Foresters Capt P.B. Coles to be Adjutant dated 25/3/15	
	18 to 21		Nothing of importance	
	22		Extract from London Gazette 5th Batt Sherwood Foresters Edward Cuzon Villa to be 2nd Lt dated 23/3/15	
	23 to 30		Nothing of importance.	

1875 Wt. W593/826 1,000,000 4/15 J.B.C. & A. A.D.S.S./Forms/C. 2118.

Confidential

2/5th Sherwood Foresters

Army Form C. 2118.

WAR DIARY
or
INTELLIGENCE SUMMARY.
(*Erase heading not required.*)

Instructions regarding War Diaries and Intelligence Summaries are contained in F. S. Regs., Part II. and the Staff Manual respectively. Title pages will be prepared in manuscript.

Place	Date	Hour	Summary of Events and Information	Remarks and references to Appendices
	1915 MAY			
LUTON	5		2nd Lt G B Robotham having joined BEF struck off strength on & from 1/5/15	[illegible]
	6		Extract from London Gazette 5th Batt Sherwood Forester 2nd Lt A L Rose to be Tempy Capt dated 16/4/15	[illegible]
	10		2nd Lt R C S Bennett having joined BEF struck off strength on & from 8/5/15. 2nd Lts F G Robinson + [illegible] Sutherland transferred to 3/5th Batt Sherwood Foresters & struck off strength	[illegible]
	15		Extract from London Gazette 5th Batt Sherwood Foresters Howard Hurley [illegible] to be 2nd Lt dated 5/5/15	[illegible]
	19		" " " " " William Geoffrey Wright Barber to be 2nd Lt dated 12/2/15.	[illegible]
	20		Two Jap Rifles Bayonets vouchered to O/C 2/1 NMD Cyclist Co.	[illegible]

G. C. Aitchison Lt Col

T2134. Wt. W708–776. 500000. 4/15. Sir J. C. & S.

Confidential

Instructions regarding War Diaries and Intelligence Summaries are contained in F. S. Regs., Part II. and the Staff Manual respectively. Title pages will be prepared in manuscript.

WAR DIARY
or
INTELLIGENCE SUMMARY.
(Erase heading not required.)

2/5th Sherwood Foresters

Army Form C. 2118.

Place	Date	Hour	Summary of Events and Information	Remarks and references to Appendices
	1915 JUNE			
LUTON	2		163 Jap Rifles + Bayonets returned to O.O Tower of London	[illegible]
	4		The Battn moved by road into Camp at Dunstable under the command of Capt F.E.W. Donne. Home service officers + men remained in Luton being formed into a Provisional Battn	[illegible]
DUNSTABLE	11		9 officers + 553 other ranks transferred to 9th Northern Home Battn.	[illegible]
	22		Officers Saddlery received	[illegible]
	24		Field firing commenced	[illegible]
	30		Extract from London Gazette 5th Battn Sherwood Foresters Alfred Tatam Prince to be 2nd Lt dated 5/6/15	[illegible]

G. A. Hutchinson [illegible]

Confidential

2/5th Sherwood Foresters

Army Form C. 2118.

Instructions regarding War Diaries and Intelligence Summaries are contained in F. S. Regs., Part II. and the Staff Manual respectively. Title pages will be prepared in manuscript.

WAR DIARY
or
INTELLIGENCE SUMMARY.

(Erase heading not required.)

Place	Date	Hour	Summary of Events and Information	Remarks and references to Appendices
DUNSTABLE	1915 JULY 1		2nd Lt. F H Sutherland transferred from 3/5th Batt Sherwood Foresters & taken on strength 26/6/15 3 N.C.Os & 98 men attached to C company transferred from 3/5th Batt & taken on strength 26/6/15	GA
	5		Harness universal received	GA
	13		2nd Lts E.F. Ann F.L. Bailey J. E. McInnes W.G. Barber + H.S. Downton transferred to 1/5th Batt and struck off strength 11/7/15	GA
	14		Major G. C. Aitchison 2/8th Batt Sherwood Foresters arrived & assumed temporary command of the Batt pending his Gazette to that appointment. 9 G.S.L. Wagons received	GA
	16		2nd Lt. K Benrose transferred to 1/5th Batt and struck off strength 15/7/15	GA
	21		Inspection of Batt by the Brigade Commander	GA
	24		Extract from London Gazette 5th Sherwood Foresters Regt Q M S Joseph Farnsworth from 6th Batt Sherwood Foresters to be Quartermaster with honorary rank of Lt dated 25/5/15	GA
	31		Extract from London Gazette 5th Sherwood Foresters Major G.C. Aitchison to be Lt. Colonel (Tempy) dated 28/7/15.	GA

G. C. Aitchison / Lt Col

1577 Wt. W10791/1773 500,000 1/15 D. D. & L. A.D.S.S./Forms/C. 2118.

Confidential

2/5th Sherwood Foresters

Army Form C. 2118.

Instructions regarding War Diaries and Intelligence Summaries are contained in F. S. Regs., Part II. and the Staff Manual respectively. Title pages will be prepared in manuscript.

WAR DIARY

or

INTELLIGENCE SUMMARY.

(Erase heading not required.)

Place	Date	Hour	Summary of Events and Information	Remarks and references to Appendices
DUNSTABLE	1915 AUGUST 3		2nd Lts E.B. Woodforde + E.C. Villa transferred to 1/5th Batt + struck off strength on this date	[initials]
	4		Extract from London Gazette 5th Batt Sherwood Foresters. Cadet Herbert Waterhouse from the Sheffield Univ Contingent Senior Division O.T.C to be 2nd Lt dated 21/4/15.	[initials]
	9		The Batt moved by road into Cassiobury Park Camp at WATFORD	[initials]
WATFORD	31		2nd Lt. H Binks taken on strength of the Batt today.	[initials]

[signature] Lt Col

Confidential

2/5th Sherwood Foresters

Army Form C. 2118

Instructions regarding War Diaries and Intelligence Summaries are contained in F. S. Regs., Part II. and the Staff Manual respectively. Title Pages will be prepared in manuscript.

WAR DIARY
or
INTELLIGENCE SUMMARY
(Erase heading not required.)

Place	Date 1915	Hour	Summary of Events and Information	Remarks and references to Appendices
WATFORD	September 1		Four Field Kitchens Travelling received	
	15		Inspection by G.O.C 59th N.M. Division in Gorhambury Park St Albans	
	24		8 sets Pack Saddlery received	
	24		Inspection of Transport by Lt Col E. G. Reading A.S.C	
	30		Inspection of arms & equipment by the Brigade Commander	

G. C. Aitchison Lt Col

1875 Wt. W593/826 1,000,000 4/15 J.B.C. & A. A.D.S.S./Forms/C. 2118.

CONFIDENTIAL.

Statement to accompany War Diary, for the Month of

September, 1915.

There has been little of importance to record during the month. The Battalion has remained under canvas, , the weather has been favourable, and the health of the men generally good, with the exception of Scabies, which has been prevalent.

ADMINISTRATION   MEDICAL SERVICES

The appointment of a permanent M.O. for the Battalion, is I consider, an important and urgent matter.

G. P. Aitchison

Lieut-Colonel,

Cmm'g 2/5th Battalion, The Sherwood Foresters.

2/5 Sherwood Foresters

Army Form C. 2118.

WAR DIARY
or
~~INTELLIGENCE SUMMARY.~~

(Erase heading not required.)

Instructions regarding War Diaries and Intelligence Summaries are contained in F. S. Regs., Part II. and the Staff Manual respectively. Title pages will be prepared in manuscript.

Place	Date 1915	Hour	Summary of Events and Information	Remarks and references to Appendices
Watford (Camp)	October 1st		The Battalion marched, with the Brigade, to Gorhambury Park, St Albans, where it was inspected by the G.O.C. in C. (Gen. Sir Leslie Rundle) & returned to Camp after the Inspection	
	2nd		O.C. Companies made their own arrangements for Pay, foot & Kit inspections. The M.O. held a Medical Inspection. No training could be done owing to the state of the weather. The Battalion found Brigade duties	
	3rd		Sunday. Church parade, on the Brigade Parade Ground	
	4th		The Battalion proceeded to Moor Park for digging and entrenching. "B" Company fired a course on the Miniature Range & carried out Musketry and Bayonet fighting. "C" Company sent a Bomb Throwing party for instruction. The following is an extract from the London Gazette:- 7th Sept 1915 Capt. F.E.M. Donne to be temp. Major dated 19.8.15 8th " " 2nd Lieut. Nadin to be Adjutant dated 13.8.15. 13th " " 2nd Lieut. F.H.L. Stibbing to be temp. Captain dated 13.7.15 23rd " " Pte. W.H. Chandler from Inns of Court O.T.C. to be 2nd Lieut. dated 23.8.15. 25th " " Sgt. H.A.J. Hayhoe to be 2nd Lieut. dated 7.9.15.	
	5th		All men who had not been vaccinated paraded for Musketry, Bayonet Fighting and Miniature Range. The Army Act, secs. 4 to 44 inclusive and para. 461 K.R's. were read to all men. 3 new blankets were issued to each man and the old ones withdrawn	
	6th		The Battalion took part in Divisional Field Operations, taking up a defensive position on Serches Farm	
	7th		The Battalion carried out Field Training. At night it proceeded to Moor Park for manning & relieving trenches	
	8th		In the morning A Battalion Route March. In the afternoon: Kit & Medical Inspections	

2353 Wt. W2514/1454 700,000 5/15 D. D. & L. A.D.S.S./Forms/C. 2118.

Army Form C. 2118.

Instructions regarding War Diaries and Intelligence Summaries are contained in F. S. Regs., Part II. and the Staff Manual respectively. Title pages will be prepared in manuscript.

WAR DIARY

~~or~~

~~INTELLIGENCE SUMMARY.~~

(*Erase heading not required.*)

Place	Date 1915	Hour	Summary of Events and Information	Remarks and references to Appendices
Watford (Camp)	October 9th		Close Order drill, both Battalion and Company, was carried out in Cassiobury Park	
	10th		Sunday: Church Parade on the Brigade Parade Ground.	
	11th		Trench digging was carried out by the Battalion in Moor Park. 2nd Lt A.G. Prince was detailed to attend a course of instruction at Ongar, commencing on the 15th inst.	
	12th		The Battalion proceeded to the Bayonet Fighting Course in Cassiobury Park and repaired it. "B" Coy. paraded for Miniature Range, Musketry & Bayonet Exercises. "C" Company sent a bomb throwing party for instruction	
	13th		The Battalion took part in Divisional Field Operations practising taking cover from aerial observation, covering a right flank of a main body which was protecting a convoy and taking up positions at Serches Farm, Whitehouse Farm & Serches Hill. 2nd Lieut. G Nutt proceeded overseas to join the 1/5th Battn	
	14th		The Battalion paraded for close order drill and bayonet fighting. "C" Company paraded for Miniature Range and Musketry and sent a party for instruction in bomb throwing.	
	15th		In the morning: A battalion route march. In the afternoon: Pay, Kit & medical inspections. All casuals fired on the Miniature Range	
	16th		Close order drill & field training was carried out by the Battalion in Cassiobury Park. "D" Coy. paraded for Musketry, Miniature Range & Bayonet fighting.	
	17th		Sunday. Church Parade on the Brigade Parade Ground	
	18th		Camp was struck and the Battalion moved into billets	
	19th		The Battalion proceeded to Cassiobury Park & cleaned up & put in order the old camp site.	
	20th		The Battalion proceeded to Callowland & commenced digging & making a new Bayonet Fighting Course	
	21st		The Battalion took part in Brigade Field Operations.	

2353 Wt. W2544/1454 700,000 5/15 D. D. & L. A.D.S.S./Forms/C. 2118.

Army Form C. 2118.

WAR DIARY

or

~~INTELLIGENCE SUMMARY.~~

(Erase heading not required.)

Instructions regarding War Diaries and Intelligence Summaries are contained in F. S. Regs., Part II. and the Staff Manual respectively. Title pages will be prepared in manuscript.

Place	Date 1915	Hour	Summary of Events and Information	Remarks and references to Appendices
Watford	October 22nd		In the morning: A Battalion route march. In the afternoon: Pay: Kit + medical inspections. The Battalion was on Brigade duty.	
	23rd		The Battalion carried out general training and close order drill on Callowland.	
	25th		The Battalion carried out entrenching on the Bayonet Fighting Course at Callowland. "A" Coy. paraded for Miniature Range + Musketry. Bomb throwing parties were detailed for the week. 2nd Lt W.H. Chandler detailed to attend an elementary course at The Barracks, Hertford commencing on this day. 2nd Lieut. W.B. Allibon detailed to attend a Course of Instruction at the Staff College which commences this day.	
	26th		The Battalion proceeded to Black Boy Wood to take part in a scheme of wood fighting with the 2/8th Battalion. A defensive position in the wood was taken up as a rear guard protecting the passage of the River Colne.	
	27th		The Battalion carried out Bayonet Fighting, Physical Drill + Musketry on Callowland. At night the Battn marched to Moor Park for night digging and improving the trenches.	
	28th		Lectures were delivered under Company arrangements. 2nd Lieuts. S.S. Milner + H.S. Keane joined for duty.	
	29th		The Battalion paraded for a route march. Men who had not fired a course on the open range paraded for special firing instruction.	
	30th		The Battalion paraded + proceeded to Callowland for close order drill and bayonet fighting. Sergt. R. Lees was detailed to attend a grenadier course at Godstone commencing on 3rd Novr 1915	
	31st		The Battalion paraded for Divine Service in the Central Hall. The address was given by the Rt. Rev. the Lord Bishop of Southwell	

2353 Wt. W2544/1454 700,000 5/15 D. D. & L. A.D.S.S./Forms/C. 2118.

2/5th Sherwood Foresters

CONFIDENTIAL.

STATEMENT TO ACCOMPANY THE WAR DIARY FOR THE MONTH OF OCTOBER 1915.

During the month the Battalion has moved out of Camp into Billets.

TRAINING.

Practically the whole of the men in this Battalion have been in training for over a year. If endeavours were made to vary the work and introduce, as far as possible, new features it would make it more interesting for the men.

ADMINISTRATION. MEDICAL SERVICES.

The appointment of Lieut. S.O. Bingham R.A.M.C. as Medical Officer has been of great benefit to the Battalion, which was for so long a time without a permanent Medical Officer.

SUPPLY SERVICES.

Owing, I am informed, to a shortage of horses in the A.S.C. the Regimental Transport has for some time been drawing practically the whole of the rations and forage for this Battalion in addition to their other work.

TRANSPORT SERVICES.

I consider that the L.D.horses which are doing the work of H.D. horses should be foraged as H.D. horses.

BILLETING.

The billets occupied by the Battalion are good. I find that the practice of sleeping part of the Battalion in schools and the remainder in billets leads to a certain amount of dissatisfaction.

MISCELLANEOUS.

I have still been unable to obtain promotion for my Officers and I consider that this is a pressing and urgent matter.

I find that the provision of the numerous parties, picquets, duties and guards presses very heavily on the men who therefore have very little time for rest and recreation. Frequently the same men have to be detailed for one of the above duties on three consecutive nights.

COURSES.

Whilst recognising the importance of Officers and N.C.O's. attending courses of instruction, if arrangements could be made to avoid so many being away from the Battalion at the same time the work and training of the Battalion would not be so interfered with as at present.

G C Aitchison

Lieut.Colonel,
Cmm'g. 2/5th. Battalion,
The Sherwood Foresters.

WATFORD.

7th. November 1915.

Army Form C. 2118.

Instructions regarding War Diaries and Intelligence Summaries are contained in F. S. Regs., Part II. and the Staff Manual respectively. Title pages will be prepared in manuscript.

WAR DIARY
or
~~INTELLIGENCE SUMMARY~~.
(Erase heading not required.)

Place	Date 1915	Hour	Summary of Events and Information	Remarks and references to Appendices
WATFORD	November 1		"D" Company moved out of billets into PARKGATE ROAD School	
	2		Nothing of importance	
	3		The Battalion took part in Brigade Field Operations	
	4		The Battalion proceeded to MOOR PARK in the afternoon and took part in an attack with bombs against trenches before the G.O.C.	
	5		Nothing of importance	
	6		ditto	
	7		About 10.15 pm a message that hostile aircraft were in the district was received & the Battalion which was on Brigade duties stood to and all guards & parties fell in at their respective posts	
	8		Nothing of importance	
	9		The Battalion took part in Divisional Field Operations forming part of the RED FORCE. The Battalion was allotted frontage on the right of the line with orders to protect same with the support of a Battery of R.F.A. Later orders were received for a general advance the Battalion to change direction N.N.W; the 2/5th South Staffordshires opposed our advance. Weather very inclement.	
	10		The Battalion paraded in Callowland and were inspected in Bayonet fighting, Musketry, Close Order Drill Physical Drill and Extended Order Drill by Major General Dickson Inspector of Infantry	
	11		41 men fired a Short Japanese Course (10 Rounds) on Chalk Hill Range St. Albans	
	12		Nothing of importance	
	13		ditto	
	14		ditto	
	15		ditto	
	16		The G.O.C. inspected the Battalion in CASSIOBURY PARK including the 1st Line Transport 154,000 rounds .303 Mark VI Ammunition received	

2353 Wt. W2514/1454 700,000 5/15 D. D. & L. A.D.S.S./Forms/C. 2118.

Instructions regarding War Diaries and Intelligence Summaries are contained in F. S. Regs., Part II. and the Staff Manual respectively. Title pages will be prepared in manuscript.

WAR DIARY
or
~~INTELLIGENCE SUMMARY.~~
(Erase heading not required.)

Army Form C. 2118.

Place	Date	Hour	Summary of Events and Information	Remarks and references to Appendices
WATFORD	November 14		The Battalion took part in a Brigade Route March. No casualties	
	18		The Battalion paraded at 5 pm for 6 hours night digging. The trenches dug were good and the men were well under cover in two hours time	
	19		Nothing of importance	
	20		ditto	
	21		540 M L M Rifles were received and afterwards issued	
	22		Japanese Ammunition Rifles and accessories returned to WEEDON	
	23		a Bombing Party took part in a display before the G.O.C in MOOR PARK	
	24		Nothing of importance	
	25		The Battalion took part in a Divisional Route March to Leverstock Green. No casualties Extract from Gazette 2nd Lt Trafford Kaan to be temp Capt & Lorman Adjutant dated 15/10/15. The undermentioned 2nd Lts to be temp Lts dated 15/10/15 C. G. Claye, H.D.M. Wright, F.W. Smith, G. H. Williamson, F.H. Sutherland W.B. Allison	
	26		Nothing of importance	
	27		ditto	
	28		ditto	
	29		"C & D" Companies commenced a special course of company training for 3 weeks	
	30		Nothing of importance	

[illegible initials]

2353 Wt. W2544/1454 700,000 5/15 D. D. & L. A.D.S.S./Forms/C. 2118.

2/5th. Battalion. The Sherwood Foresters.

CONFIDENTIAL.

STATEMENT TO ACCOMPANY THE WAR DIARY FOR THE MONTH OF NOVEMBER 1915.

Training.

On the 29th. of the month two Companies commenced a special course of Company training for three weeks under their Company Commanders.

The scheme has my hearty approval and I am very hopeful of the results that will ensue. I regret that junior officers should have been withdrawn from their Companies during this special training to attend courses as they have been prevented from receiving instruction in commanding their own platoons..

During the month the Japanese rifles were withdrawn and Lee Metford rifles substituted. I consider that this exchange is very unfortunate as it is impossible to instruct the men in rapid loading and firing owing to the fact that the Lee Metford rifles are not "charger loaders". The rifles are of an old date and generally faulty.

Supply Services.

The Regimental Transport has continued during the month to draw the rations and forage for the Battalion in addition to their ordinary Regimental Transport work.

Transport Services.

The horses have been in stables and are in very good condition and free from sickness and disease.

G.S.limbered wagons have been withdrawn and replaced by G.S.Wagons; this, I presume, is only a temporary measure, if not I consider that long rein driving should be substituted for "ride and drive".

Ordnance Services.

There has been an improvement in the supply of stores from D.A.D.O.S. during the month.

Nothing whatever has been supplied by O. i/c Barracks during the month.

Billetting.

No change has been made during the month in the billetting of the Battalion. Where men are accommodated in schools or similar hired buildings I consider that, having regard to the time of year, some provision should be made for drying clothes if the health of the Battalion is not to suffer.

Miscellaneous.

Central messing is working well and the cooking of meals under present conditions is good and giving general satisfaction. It has been difficult to serve meals properly owing to no plates and mugs having been supplied.

No alteration was made during the month in the provision of parties, duties and fatigues but December orders have rectified this.

G. C. Aitchison

Lieut.Colonel,
Cmm'g. 2/5th. Battalion,
The Sherwood Foresters.

WATFORD,
7th. December 1915.

Subject :- War Diaries.

From Officer Commanding,

2/5th Bn. Sherwood Foresters.

To Headquarters,

178th Infantry Brigade.

With reference to your letters 1271/9 of 23rd Nov.'15, and 28th Nov.'15 ;

There are no records in possession of this Battalion prior to

1st April, 1915 as regards clothing.

1st Nov. 1914 as regards equipment.

It is therefore impossible for me to give any further information than that obtainable from the copies of Battalion Orders in my possession, and information supplied by Major F.E.M.Donne who was at Long Eaton and sent recruits to Derby in batches in civilian clothing.

G. C. Aitchison

Lieut-Colonel,
Cmm'g 2/5th Battn.
The Sherwood Foresters.

Watford,

28/11/15.

Army Form C. 2118

Instructions regarding War Diaries and Intelligence Summaries are contained in F. S. Regs., Part II. and the Staff Manual respectively. Title Pages will be prepared in manuscript.

WAR DIARY
or
~~INTELLIGENCE SUMMARY~~

(Erase heading not required.)

Place	Date 1915	Hour	Summary of Events and Information	Remarks and references to Appendices
WATFORD	December 1		The Battalion took part in a Brigade Route March which was eventually abandoned owing to inclement weather	
	2		Nothing of importance	
	3		ditto	
	4		ditto	
	5		ditto	
	6		ditto	
	7		ditto	
	8		Battalion Headquarters Staff engaged on Administrative Scheme. Battalion Route March (20 miles)	
	9		ditto ditto	
	10		ditto ditto	
	11		Nothing of importance	
	12		ditto	
	13		"A" Company moved into new area out of billets. System of sleeping in large empty buildings now adopted throughout Battn	
	14		"B" Company moved into new area. C.O attended conference on Administrative Scheme at Div. H.Qs.	
	15		Brigade Route March cancelled owing to inclement weather	
	16		Headquarters & Q.M's Stores moved into new area. First Special Leave Party 10% of Establishment	
	17		Nothing of importance	
	18		"C" Company moved into new area	
	19		Nothing of importance	
	20		"C" & "D" companies completed Special Company Training & were inspected by the Brigade Commander in Cassiobury Park. "D" Company moved into new area	
	21		The Battalion took part in a Divisional Route March forming the Advance Guard of the Sherwood Foresters Brigade. Second Special Leave party.	
	22		Nothing of importance	
	23		ditto	

1875 Wt. W593/826 1,000,000 4/15 J.B.C. & A. A.D.S.S./Forms/C. 2118.

Instructions regarding War Diaries and Intelligence Summaries are contained in F. S. Regs., Part II. and the Staff Manual respectively. Title Pages will be prepared in manuscript.

WAR DIARY

or

~~INTELLIGENCE SUMMARY~~

(Erase heading not required.)

Army Form C. 2118

Place	Date	Hour	Summary of Events and Information	Remarks and references to Appendices
WATFORD	December 24		Nothing of importance	
	25		Xmas Day	
	26		Third special leave party	
	27		General holiday	
	28		Nothing of importance	
	29		ditto	
	30		Battalion Route March.	
	31		Fourth Special leave party. Following officers transferred to 3/5th Sherwood Foresters and struck off strength from this date Capt J. H. Winning 2nd Lt J. B. Farrington 2nd Lt. W. Hebbert & 2nd Lt W.H. Chandler. Last mentioned officer remains attached	

1875 Wt. W593/826 1,000,000 4/15 J.B.C. & A. A.D.S.S./Forms/C. 2118.

CONFIDENTIAL.

2/5th. Battalion, The Sherwood Foresters.

STATEMENT TO ACCOMPANY THE WAR DIARY FOR THE MONTH OF DECEMBER 1915.

TRAINING.

The Special course of Company training was completed on the 20th. of the month by "C" &"D" Companies. Despite the difficulties entailed by the very inclement weather I consider that the training was of the greatest benefit to officers, N.C.O's. and men and there has been a considerable increase in general efficiency and discipline in the Companies concerned.

Owing to the small numbers of the Battalion very little training could be carried out with "A" & "B" Companies who found all details, employed men, guards and fatigues for the Battalion during the period of Special Company training.

This will apply to "C" & "D" Companies next month when "A" & "B" Companies commence their Special Training.

The speedy issue of modern rifles is, I consider, of great importance for the reasons appearing in my last monthly statement.

SUPPLY SERVICES.

The A.S.C. have not drawn rations and forage for the Battalion during the month and as G.S.limbered wagons have recently been issued to replace G.S.Wagons in possession the question becomes a matter of real urgency as the G.S.L.wagons may not be used for that purpose.

ORDNANCE SERVICES.

Before moving into the new area absolute essentials were supplied by Officer i/c. Barracks but there are still a considerable quantity of really necessary articles of which I am unable to obtain delivery, e.g., wash basins, drinking mugs, brooms and brushes

BILLETING.

The Battalion has moved into a new area and the Central Sleeping system is now in force.

Large empty houses have been secured which, in my opinion, are preferable to schools or skating rinks.

Suggestions were invited as to the provision of an extra supply of coal for drying of clothes when necessary but nothing has yet resulted.

Several of the houses are very dilapidated and I am somewhat apprehensive of trouble arising on that account. In other cases men are quartered in rooms with light wall papers and white paint and, even with the greatest care, some damage must inevitably ensue and cannot, in my opinion, be fairly charged against the men. The exceptional size of the plate and ordinary glass windows in some of these rooms becomes a most serious financial burden on the men in the event of a pane being broken approximately 6 or 7 weeks pay in case of a breakage.

MISCELLANEOUS.

The Messing Committee for the Battalion has been formed but as the system has only been adopted as from 1.1.'16 I defer making any comments until next month.

G. C. Aitchison

Lieut.Colonel,
Cmm'g. 2/5th. Battalion,
The Sherwood Foresters.

WATFORD,

7th. January 1916.

Subject. War Diary.

From Headquarters.
178th. Infantry Brigade.
Watford.

To O.C.
2/5th. Battalion.
Sherwood Foresters.

Will you please inform me for the purposes of the Brigade War Diary how many men left your Battalion during the month of November 1915 stating opposite each set of numbers where they went e.g. To Provisional Battalion, Discharged, Joined other Units, struck off as Deserter and so on.

If you will kindly furnish this information each month I shall be obliged.

Capt.
Brigade Major.
178th. Infantry Brigade.

Watford.
15/12/15.

From:-O.C. 2/5th. Battalion,
The Sherwood Foresters.

To:- Headquarters,
178th. Infantry Brigade.

The numbers are as follows:-

To Provisional Battalion	19	
To 3/5th. Battn. Sherwood Foresters	1	x
To 3/6th. " " "	1	÷
To Northants Yeomanry	4	M.M.P.
Struck off as deserter	1	
	26	

x. Physical Training Instructor

÷ Permanent Staff Warrant Officer

G. C. Aitchison

Lieut.Colonel

(13)

Confidential

War Diary

of

2/5th Batt. Sherwood Foresters.

From 1st to 31st January 1916

Volume XV

Confidential

2/5th Sherwood Foresters.

Army Form C. 2118

WAR DIARY
or
~~INTELLIGENCE SUMMARY~~
(Erase heading not required.)

Instructions regarding War Diaries and Intelligence Summaries are contained in F. S. Regs., Part II. and the Staff Manual respectively. Title Pages will be prepared in manuscript.

Place	Date 1916	Hour	Summary of Events and Information	Remarks and references to Appendices
WATFORD	JANUARY 6		"A" and "B" Companies commence Special Company Training	
	18		Inspection of Machine Gun Section at St Albans by G.O.C. 59th N.M. Division	
	22		First draft of recruits arrived today (15 men)	
	26		100 Rifles M.L.E. C.L. III* Short received	
	28		Extract from London Gazette Capt R.B. RICKMAN to be temporary Major dated 3/1/16	
	29		"A" and "B" Companies completed Special Company Training having been inspected by the Brigade Commander	
	31		Zeppelin Raid reported. The Battn stood-by in billets not being on duty or trust for duty. Number of Recruits received to date 120.	

G. C. Aitchison Lt Col

CONFIDENTIAL.

2/5th. Battalion, The Sherwood Foresters.

STATEMENT TO ACCOMPANY THE WAR DIARY FOR THE MONTH OF JANUARY 1916.

TRAINING.

The Special Course of Company training was completed on the 29th. of the month by "A" & "B" Compaies.

I have rendered a separate report upon this training so do not allude further to it in this statement.

100 Short L.E. rifles have been received and I trust that the whole Battalion will shortly be armed with similar rifles and thus enable the men to obtain a proper knowledge of the weapon that they will take abroad.

The firing of a course of musketry is, I consider, of great importance.

ORDNANCE SERVICES.

The supply of stores by O. i/c. Barracks has been much improved during the month.

MISCELLANEOUS.

The shortage of officers available for ordinary company work and duties is a serious matter. At the present moment one Company Commander has no subaltern and two Company commanders have only one subaltern each available for duty with their companies and the best N.C.O's. are being withdrawn for the training of recruits. Unless the establishment of officers is increased I fail to see how the position is to be improved. Courses, special duties and occasional sickness are a heavy drain on the minimum number at present allowed.

MESSING.

The inauguration of the new system has entailed a considerable amount of work but it is beginning to run smoothly. There is no doubt that the men are better fed.

G. C. Aitchison

Lieut.Colonel, Cmm'g.

2/5th. Bn. Sherwood Foresters.

WATFORD.

5th. February 1916

14

Confidential

War Diary

of

2/5th Batt. Sherwood Foresters.

From 1st to 29th February 1916.

Volume XVI

Confidential

2/5th Sherwood Foresters

Army Form C. 2118

Instructions regarding War Diaries and Intelligence Summaries are contained in F. S. Regs., Part II. and the Staff Manual respectively. Title Pages will be prepared in manuscript.

WAR DIARY
or
~~INTELLIGENCE SUMMARY~~

(Erase heading not required.)

Place	Date 1916	Hour	Summary of Events and Information	Remarks and references to Appendices
WATFORD	January 2.		Inspection in Route March by G.O.C III Army	[illegible]
	12 & 15		Muster parades of the Battalion held	[illegible]
	19		23rd & final draft of recruits received. Total number received during month 252	[illegible]
	22		Inspection of recruits by G.O.C. 59 N.M. Division	[illegible]
	29		Battalion ordered to move on Emergency Scheme B (Test only)	[illegible]

G. C. Aitchison Lt Col

1875 Wt. W593/826 1,000,000 4/15 J.B.C. & A. A.D.S.S./Forms/C. 2118.

CONFIDENTIAL.

2/5th Battalion, The Sherwood Foresters.

Statement to accompany the War Diary for the month of February 1916.

TRAINING.

The full number of recruits required have been received during the month. Taken as a whole they are a good stamp of men, and their training is progressing satisfactorily , though the inclement weather during the latter part of the month has been a considerable drawback.

Musketry.

No opportunity has yet been given for firing those men who have not completed a course of Musketry.

MISCELLANEOUS.

The shortage of Officers is still a serious matter. Application has been made to the Third Line for the required number to complete establishment but none have yet arrived .

G. C. Aitchison

Lieut-Colonel,
Cmm'g 2/5th Battalion,
The Sherwood Foresters.

Watford,

7/3/16.

WO 3025
59th DIV

2-5th BN NOTTS + DERBY
Regt

1917 - Feb - 1918 July

59TH DIVISION
178TH INFY BDE

2-5TH BN NOTTS & DERBY REGT

FEB 1917 - ~~JUN~~ JLY 1918

DISBANDED

Confidential

Instructions regarding War Diaries and Intelligence Summaries are contained in F. S. Regs., Part II. and the Staff Manual respectively. Title Pages will be prepared in manuscript.

WAR DIARY
or
~~INTELLIGENCE SUMMARY~~

(Erase heading not required.)

Army Form C. 2118.

Battn
2/5th Notts & Derbyshire Regt
FEBRUARY 1917

178/9

Vol 1

Place	Date	Hour	Summary of Events and Information	Remarks and references to Appendices
	FEBRUARY			
HURDCOTT	23		First Line Transport + Detachment of 3 Officers + 88 O.R left HURDCOTT for FRANCE proceeding via SOUTHAMPTON to HAVRE	[initials]
"	24		Major G H St HILL assumed command of Battn vice Lt Col G C AITCHISON	[initials]
"	25		Battn 23 Officers 868 O.R left HURDCOTT for FRANCE	[initials]
FOLKESTONE BOULOGNE	26		Battn arrived FOLKESTONE 5 am. Embarked 2 pm + disembarked BOULOGNE 5 pm + proceeded to Rest Camp.	[initials]
VERS	27		Bn entrained BOULOGNE 9 am + arrived SALEUX 3.30 pm. Billeted at VERS for night	[initials]
St FUCIEN	28		Bn proceeded by Route March to St FUCIEN where First Line Transport + party joined. Billeted at St FUCIEN for night	[initials]

G. H. St Hill Major
Cmdg. 2/5 Notts & Derby Regt

1.25

Confidential

Instructions regarding War Diaries and Intelligence Summaries are contained in F. S. Regs., Part II. and the Staff Manual respectively. Title Pages will be prepared in manuscript.

WAR DIARY
or
~~INTELLIGENCE SUMMARY~~

MARCH 1917

(Erase heading not required.)

Army Form C. 2118.

2/5th Battn. Notts + Derby Regt

Vol II

Place	Date MARCH	Hour	Summary of Events and Information	Remarks and references to Appendices
	1.		Battn proceeded by Route March to WARFUSEE - ABANCOURT + were billeted in hutments	Ty
	9		Battn proceeded by Route March to FOUCAUCOURT + billeted in hutments + dug outs	Ty
	21		Battn proceeded by Route March to + relieved 1st Battn NORTHANTS REGT occupying abandoned German Trenches E of BRIE viz BINGEN TRENCH O29 NASSAU TRENCH O28 and ULM TRENCH O34 (Ref. FRANCE 62c SW 1/20000). One company detached in outpost duty at MONS-EN-CHAUSSEE P27 (Ref FRANCE 62c SE 1/20.000)	Ty
	22		Consolidation of trenches to form BRIE Bridge Head commenced	Ty
	23		Battn relieved by 2/4th Battn Notts + Derby Regt in all trenches S of BRIE - MONS-EN-CHAUSSEE Road 4th Battn Royal BERKS on left of Battn	Ty
	26		Battn proceeded by route march to VRAIGNES + billeted in evacuated houses One company detached at HANCOURT with outposts at BERNES + FLECHIN One platoon in outpost at POEUILLY billeted in ruined houses + cellars	Ty
	28		Battn proceeded by route march to FLECHIN + commenced construction of line of Cruciform Posts. Outpost at BERNES withdrawn + relieved by 2/4th Bn NOTTS + DERBY Regt	Ty

G.H. [illegible] Lieut Col.

2449 Wt. W14957/M90 750,000 1/16 J.B.C. & A. Forms/C.2118/12.

Confidential

I

WAR DIARY
or
~~INTELLIGENCE SUMMARY~~

(Erase heading not required.)

Instructions regarding War Diaries and Intelligence Summaries are contained in F. S. Regs., Part II. and the Staff Manual respectively. Title Pages will be prepared in manuscript.

Army Form C. 2118.

2/5th Battn SHERWOOD FORESTERS

Vol 3

Place	Date APRIL	Hour 1917	Summary of Events and Information	Remarks and references to Appendices
FLECHIN	3		The Battn proceeded by route march to VENDELLES	
VENDELLES	4		An attack launched on village of LE VERGUIER (Copy operation orders attached) The attacking troops came under heavy shell and concealed M.G. fire & were eventually compelled under cover of a snowstorm to fall back on to their original positions. Casualties Killed 1 Officer 19 O.R. Wounded 4 Officers 80 O.R.	
	7		The Battn relieved 2/7th Battn SHERWOOD FORESTERS in the line	
	9		At 6am the Division on our R reported that the enemy had evacuated the trenches in R5 & R12. The 184th Inf Brigade pushed forward patrols & occupied these trenches. At 9am the Battn Snipers & Bombers penetrated into LE VERGUIER and found it unoccupied. Two companies advanced in support and moved to N end of the village remaining 2 companies moved to German trench in L34. R4 & R5. Consolidation of the line commenced by digging of line of rifle pits from L28 a. 9.5 through COPSE at L28 d 0.0 to L34 b 2 0 L34 d. 6.0 and on to approximately R5 a. 6.4. Casualties Killed 8 O.R. Wounded 1 Officer 11 OR	Map References FRANCE Sheets 62c NE + 62c SE 1/20000.
	10		Consolidation of position continued. Unsuccessful attempt made to occupy ASCENSION FARM at 12 noon. Battn was relieved during night by 2/5th Battn S STAFFORDS & proceeded to BERNES being in Brigade Reserve.	

G.H. [illegible] Lieut Col
2/5 Sherwood Foresters

2449 Wt. W14957/M90 750,000 1/16 J.B.C. & A. Forms/C.2118/12.

Confidential

II

Instructions regarding War Diaries and Intelligence Summaries are contained in F. S. Regs., Part II. and the Staff Manual respectively. Title Pages will be prepared in manuscript.

WAR DIARY
or
~~INTELLIGENCE SUMMARY~~
(Erase heading not required.)

Army Form C. 2118.

2/5th Battn. SHERWOOD FORESTERS

Place	Date	Hour	Summary of Events and Information	Remarks and references to Appendices
	APRIL	1917	Continued	
HERVILLY	18		The Battn. relieved the 2/5th Battn LEICESTERS at HERVILLY (one company being billeted at HESBECOURT) becoming Brigade Support.	[illegible]
	22.		The Battn relieved the 2/8th Battn SHERWOOD FORESTERS in the line, the positions taken up being as follows. D + C companies in advanced posts in a line running approximately N+S from L14.b.9.4 to CHATEAU L23 c.8.5. B company in Support in a line L22.a.3.4 to L.16.a.4.5 and A company in reserve in CARPEZA COPSE L.15. 2/4th Battn SHERWOOD FORESTERS held remainder of Brigade frontage on our L.	[illegible]
	28		B company took over Main Line of Resistance from L4.b.0.6 to L.16.a 8.8 from 2/4th Battn SHERWOOD FORESTERS	[illegible]
			Casualties since commencement of tour of duty on 22nd 2 O.R. killed. 1 wounded; exceptionally small in view of continuous shelling by enemy. 4 Officers joined during month. Fighting strength at end of month after deducting casualties, men in hospital, sick, on courses, and detachments on Division or other employ 23 Officers 440 O.R.	[illegible]

G. H. [illegible] Lieut Col
2/5 Sherwood Foresters

2449 Wt. W14957/M90 750,000 1/16 J.B.C. & A. Forms/C.2118/12.

O P E R A T I O N   O R D E R S
by
Lieut-Colonel G.H. ST. HILL T.D.
Commanding
2/5th. Battalion, Notts & Derby Regiment.
....

Map, Ref. FRANCE SHEET 62 c N.E. &
62 c S.E.

1. The Battalion will attack and capture at 7.0 a.m. tomorrow, 4th. April, the village of LE VERGUIER and SPUR 120 to the S.E.

It will then push on to GRAND PRIEL WOODS and establish ~~XXXXXX~~ touch with a Battalion of the 177th. Infantry Brigade about L 22 Central.

2. The Battalion will parade in column of route in time to move off at 5.0 a.m., the head of the column resting on Battalion Headquarters, facing WEST in the following order:- "A", "B", "D" and "C"

The Battalion will proceed in column of route to the railway at R.8.d.1.5. where it will halt.

Lieut. A.J.KAINE will lead the Battalion to this point. "A" Company will then wheel to the left and proceed in Artillery Formation in the direction indicated by Lieut. KAINE, who willlead No. 1 Platoon. "B" and "D" will conform.

The position prior to the attack will be South of the road running from R.3 Central to R.4.d.9.9.

Companies will ~~then~~ be in lines extended to 5 paces and 50 yards distances. "A" Coy. in front, followed by "B" and "D" Coys. "C" Coy. will be in support 200 yards behind "D" Coy. and will remain in Artillery Formation.

3. The Artillery Programme in support of the operation is as follows :-

WOOD and Strong Point in L 33.d. from 6 a.m. to 6.45 a.m.
LE VERGUIER and SPUR to the S.E. from 6 a.m. to 7 a.m.
WOODS L 28.d. from 7 a.m. to 7.15 a.m. Then lift.

4. At 6.40 a.m. the Left Platoon of "A" Coy will advance

and seize the wood and strong point in L.33 .d.

At 6.55 a.m. the attack on the village and spur will be delivered. Companies advancing in waves at 50 yards distance and extended to 5 paces. "B" Coy. will drop a platoon to hold the spur.

When the village is captured "A" Coy. will push on to establish communication with 177th. Brigade at GRAND PRIEL WOODS and to construct a Cruciform Post at L 22 .c. 0.5 9.0. (No. 1.)

"B" Coy. will dig a post at L.28 .c.6.6. (No. 2) "D" Coy. will dig a post at L 34.a.8.7. No.3). "C" Coy will dig a post at L 34.c. 8.4. These posts should be carefully selected to afford mutual support by Lewis Guns and to be slightly retired from the forward slope of the crest of the hill A Bombing Party of 12 men, under Sergt. HUTCHINSON will be detailed by O.C. "C" Coy. to work up the trench in conjunction with the remainder of the Battalion.

Lieut. G.H.WILLIAMSON willlead the party to the entrance of the trench at the strong point R 2 .b. "A" Coy will draw from Battalion Headquarters and carry 10 wire cutters.

"C" Coy. will draw picks and shovels from Battalion Head Quarters, and on the capture of the village will deliver picks and shovels to "A","B" and "D" Companies, at the No. 1,2 and 3 Cruciform Posts. 1 Platoon will commence digging No. 4 post.

R.E. Material will be brought up by carrying parties of the 2/6th. Battalion.

During the consolidation, Companies will send out patrols and endeavour to keep in touch with the enemy.

Representative officers from each Company will synchronize watches at Battalion Headquarters at 4.0 a.m. Each Company will carry 10 ground flares ready to light in the day-time for communication with aeroplanes.

They should be lit on any of our own aeroplanes sounding a KLAXON horn.

1 Bombing section and 1 Lewis Gun will be on both flanks of each Company.

Regimental Aid Post will be at Battalion Headquarters at VENDELLES. Battalion Battle Headquarters will be at Strong Point R.2.b. at 6.15 a.m., to which reports will be sent.

T. NADIN

Captain and Adjutant.

3.4.17

Confidential

Instructions regarding War Diaries and Intelligence Summaries are contained in F. S. Regs., Part II. and the Staff Manual respectively. Title Pages will be prepared in manuscript.

WAR DIARY
or
~~INTELLIGENCE SUMMARY~~
(Erase heading not required.)

Army Form C. 2118.

2/5th Batt: Sherwood Foresters.

Vol 4

Place	Date	Hour	Summary of Events and Information	Remarks and references to Appendices
	1917 1st May	10 pm	The Batt: was relieved in the front line running S. of VILLERET through L. 17 b + d, and L. 23 b and d, by the 2/6th Batt: Sherwood Foresters, and on relief proceeded to HESBECOURT (1 Coy.) and HERVILLY (3 Coys.), remaining there until the evening of Thursday 3rd May, resting and preparing for operations on that date.	Ref Map. Sheet 62C N.E.
	3rd May		The Batt: moved from billets to the places of assembly for attack on MALAKOFF and COLOGNE FARMS as detailed in Appendix I. which sets out the objectives in each case. "B" and "D" Coys. carried out the attack on MALAKOFF FM. and "A" and "C" Coys. on COLOGNE FM. Both objectives in the MALAKOFF FM. attack were captured, the position established in first objective being from L 6 a. 4560 to F 30 c. 4518, and in the second objective, a semicircular trench on the N E side of MALAKOFF FM. The enemy barrage in this attack was not very heavy, and the positions were taken with the bayonet and bombing parties, considerable casualties being inflicted on the enemy. Two wounded prisoners were taken, and our casualties were not heavy.	See Appendix I. Operation Orders No 2 d/d May 2nd/17 and Div. Map No 63.

2449 Wt. W14957/M90 750,000 1/16 J.B.C. & A. Forms/C.2118/12.

Confidential.

Instructions regarding War Diaries and Intelligence Summaries are contained in F. S. Regs., Part II. and the Staff Manual respectively. Title Pages will be prepared in manuscript.

WAR DIARY
or
~~INTELLIGENCE SUMMARY~~

(Erase heading not required.)

Army Form C. 2118.

2/5th Sherwood Foresters.

Place	Date	Hour	Summary of Events and Information	Remarks and references to Appendices
	1917 May 4th	7.30pm	artillery fire was directed on this wood. At 9 o'c our S.O.S went up from MALAKOFF FM. and about this time the enemy put down a very heavy barrage of all varieties of shells, including gas, extending as far back as the ridge in L.9.	SHW
		9.45pm	Enemy counter-attacked in considerable force (estimated 500) and swept round the right flank of our position. Both the advanced post and the first objective trench were evacuated the garrison being driven back to the sunken road in L.5 b and L 6 a. As this position was untenable in daylight a retirement was ordered to the Switch trench – (the original "jumping-off" place) and this was carried out.	
			The effective strength of the Batt on May 3rd prior to the attack was	
			Officers 35; Other Ranks 739.	
			The total casualties sustained in the attack and counter attack were about 150 killed wounded and missing.	

2449 Wt. W14957/M90 750,000 1/16 J.B.C. & A. Forms/C.2118/12.

Confidential

Instructions regarding War Diaries and Intelligence Summaries are contained in F. S. Regs., Part II. and the Staff Manual respectively. Title Pages will be prepared in manuscript.

WAR DIARY

or

~~INTELLIGENCE SUMMARY~~

(Erase heading not required.)

Army Form C. 2118.

25th Sherwood Foresters

Place	Date	Hour	Summary of Events and Information	Remarks and references to Appendices
	1917 May 5th (cont.)		The attack on COLOGNE FM. was unsuccessful, and the assaulting troops were unable to reach the first objective. The enemy barrage here, which opened about 5 minutes after ours, caused a good many casualties to our men in position for the attack in rear of the trench on E. edge of QUARRY in L.5.d. As they advanced they came under very heavy M.G and rifle fire, both frontal from the first objective (which had not come under our barrage owing to the short distance between it and the place of assembly) and enfilade. The gaps which had been cut in enemy wire were covered by M.Gs from the front as well as enfilade wire from supposed strong point at L6c.26. Only 2 a 3 men out of the 4 attacking waves reached the wire. The enemy barrage on the QUARRY was very heavy, causing casualties in the reserve platoons. The survivors of attacking party withdrew at 12.40 am. under cover of M.G. fire from 2/8th Sherwood Foresters post at L.5.d.9.4. and support from 178th Bde. T.M.B. Later they retired to W. side of N. clay heap in QUARRY and dug cover.	JHW.
	May 4th		During the day, consolidation of the MALAKOFF FM. positions was carried on under great difficulties. The first objective trench was very shallow and under enfilade fire from N. & S.	JHW
		7.30pm	A message was received from the post E. of MALAKOFF FM that enemy could be seen massing in wood A2 26 central, and	

2449 Wt. W14957/M90 750,000 1/16 J.B.C. & A. Forms/C.2118/12.

Confidential

Instructions regarding War Diaries and Intelligence Summaries are contained in F. S. Regs., Part II. and the Staff Manual respectively. Title Pages will be prepared in manuscript.

WAR DIARY
or
~~INTELLIGENCE SUMMARY~~
(Erase heading not required.)

Army Form C. 2118.

2/5th Sherwood Foresters

Place	Date	Hour	Summary of Events and Information	Remarks and references to Appendices
	1917 May 5		The Batt returned to billets at HESBECOURT and HERVILLY in support.	SHW
	May 6		Batt relieved by 2/5th Batt South Staffs. Regt and marched to VRAIGNES, occupying billets vacated by 2/5th South Staffs	Ref. Map Sheet 62c S.E. SHW.
	May 7th -14th		Batt in Divisional Reserve at VRAIGNES. Re-organisation and daily training. Draft of 86 men from Base arrived on 12th May.	SHW.
	May 15		Batt relieved 2/5th Batt Lincs. Regt in Divisional Reserve at JEANCOURT; two companies being at JEANCOURT and two at VENDELLES, the Cavalry Division having relieved the 59th Division in the front line. Working parties were found each night for work on the main line of resistance through GRAND PRIEL WOOD and E of LE VERGUIER.	Ref. Sheet 62c N E. SHW.
	May 29th	5 am	Batt: commenced move to EQUANCOURT area, marching to HAMELET.	62c N E. 57c S.E.
	30	5 am	Resumed march and camped at EQUANCOURT (V 16.b.&6.3)	
	31		Relieved 1/5th Bn. E. Lancs Regt in support at METZ-EN-COUTURE in trenches running through Q. 8d, Q 20 a + b, Q 21 a. and posts in Q 15 b. Effective Strength 31 Officers 698 Other Ranks.	SHW.

G.H. S?Hill.
Lieut. Col. Comdg.
2/5th Sherwood Foresters

2449 Wt. W14957/M90 750,000 1/16 J.B.C. & A. Forms/C.2118/12.

OPERATION ORDERS No 8.
by
Major R.B. Rickman, Commanding May 2nd. 1917
2/5th. Battalion, Notts & Derby Regiment.

= = = = = = = = = =

Ref:- Maps, Sheet 62 c N.E. & Special Divisional Map No. 63

1. INTENTION. On the night 3/4th. May the Battalion will attack MALAKOFF and COLOGNE FARMS.

2. OBJECTIVES. For the attack on MALAKOFF FARM there will be two objectives.

(i) The trench running W. of the Farm from L 6 a 28.55 to F 30 c 38.25 connecting up on the right with a bombing block which will be established on the night 2/3rd. May, by the 2/8th. Sherwood Foresters, at L 6 a 35.48.

A block will be formed on the left of this objective.

(ii) The road running on the N.E. side of MALAKOFF FARM from about F 30 c 2.1. to about F 30 c 70.45.

When this objective is taken it will be held by two posts of one complete platoon each. The remainder of the attacking force will then be withdrawn to the first objective.

The forming up place will be the switch trench in L 5 b and F 29 d.

For the attack on COLOGNE FARM there will be two objectives.

(i) The first objective will be the trench S.W. of COLOGNE FARM from L 6 c 5.2. to L 6 c 2.6.

Blocks will be formed on the right and left.

(ii) The second objective will be the trenches immediately E. of COLOGNE FARM at L 6 c 6.4. and L 6 c 5.7.

Blocks will be formed on both flanks. The block on the right will be at the junction of the two trenches at L 6 c 84.26.

The forming up place will be rear of the trench on Eastern Lip of the Quarry at L 6 c 0.3.

After the capture of the 2nd. objective O.C. Right Half Battalion (see para.3) will send a strong patrol to see if the Factory in G 1 b can be seized and held.

3. DISPOSITION. "B" and "D" Companies (Left Half Battalion) will carry out the attack on MALAKOFF FARM, and will be under the command of Captain R.C. TRENCH.

"A" and "C" Companies (Right Half Battalion) will carry out the attack on COLOGNE FARM, and will be under the command of Captain. T.H.L. STEBBING.

4. THE ATTACK. The attack will be carried out in two waves of two lines each as arranged by the commanders of the Right and Left Half Battalions respectively.

Bombers and Rifle Grenadiers will be on the flanks in order that the blocks mentioned in para. 2 may be formed immediately the objectives are captured.

5. BARRAGE. Artillery and Machine Gun Barrages are being arranged and details will be issued later.

6. ROUTE TO POSITION OF DEPLOYMENT HERVILLY - HESBECOURT (where "A" Coy. will join the Battalion)-to L 10 a 4.5. (Battle Headquarters) where Lieut. G.H. Williamson and his guides will lead Right Half Battalion to position of deployment.

Left Half Battalion will proceed to its position under its own guides.

7. BATTALION BATTLE HEADQUARTERS }
8. REGIMENTAL AID POST } Will be at L 10 a 4.5.
9. Battalion Dump }

10. ADVANCED BRIGADE HEADQUARTERS. Will be at RUELLES WOOD at L 7 d 7.7.

11. DRESS Fighting order as laid down by Division. In addition each man will carry one pick or one shovel and an extra sand-bag. Rifle Grenadiers 12 Granades each.

12. Watches will be synchronized at Battalion Headquarters HERVILLY at 6 p.m., May 3rd.
Zero will be at 11.30 p.m., May 3rd.

13. The head of the Battalion will pass N.E. exit from HERVILLY at 8 p.m. Order of March :- "C","B","D". 50 paces between platoons. Lewis Gun Wagons will be behind the leading platoon of each company. The wagons will be unloaded as quickly as possible on arrival at Battle Headquarters.

14. One Signalling N.C.O. and two Signallers only per Company will take part in the attack, unless extra men are specialy detailed by the Signalling Officer.

15. Packs and stores will be stacked in the present quarters under Company arrangements, and left in charge of sick men under the R.S.M.

16. The Rum ration will be issued as late as possible.

17. Attention is drawn to the followingpoints which should be broght to the notice of all ranks:-

(a) After passing through gaps in barbed wire, parties must at once spread out and reform their line.

(b) All deployments and movements must be performed with the greatest care and in dead silence.

(c) The importance of immediate consolidation. Under no circumstances is souvenir hunting to be allowed.

(d) Men should get as close as possible to the supporting barrage and kneel down.

(e) Bunching is to be avoided.

(f) The iron ration and Friday's ration will be carried on the men. Economy in water must be impressed, as a bottle may have to last 48 hours.

(g) All parties in captured trenches must at once protect their flanks.

(h) Positions captured must be held at all costs, as counter-attacks are to be expected.

(i) Every effort must be made to send back information.

T. NADIN,
Captain and Adjutant,
2/5th. Battalion, Notts & Derby Regiment.

ADDENDUM NO.1 to 2/5th. OPERATION ORDER NO.2.

. . . .

1. In continuation of para. 5 of Operation Order No 2, the attack will be made under cover of Artillery Barrages as shown on a copy of Special Divisional Map No. 63.

This is the only copy issued to the Battalion, and Maps No. 63 in possession of officers can be marked up from this map at Battalion Headquarters, HERVILLY.

It is improbable that any further copies of Map No. 63 can be obtained, copies of such parts of this map ~~s~~ as affects Companies must be taken from Maps issued.

2. The 175th. Machine Gun Company will fire upon -

The copse in F 30.c.9.8.

The Sugar Factory,

Copse in G 2 a.

The cutting in L 12 a,

will establish barrages through F 30 a and A 25 Central, and through G 7 a and G 7 c.

3. A contact aeroplane can be expected at 6 a.m. on 4th. May.

T. NADIN,
Captain and Adjutant,
2/5th. Battalion, Notts & Derby Regiment.

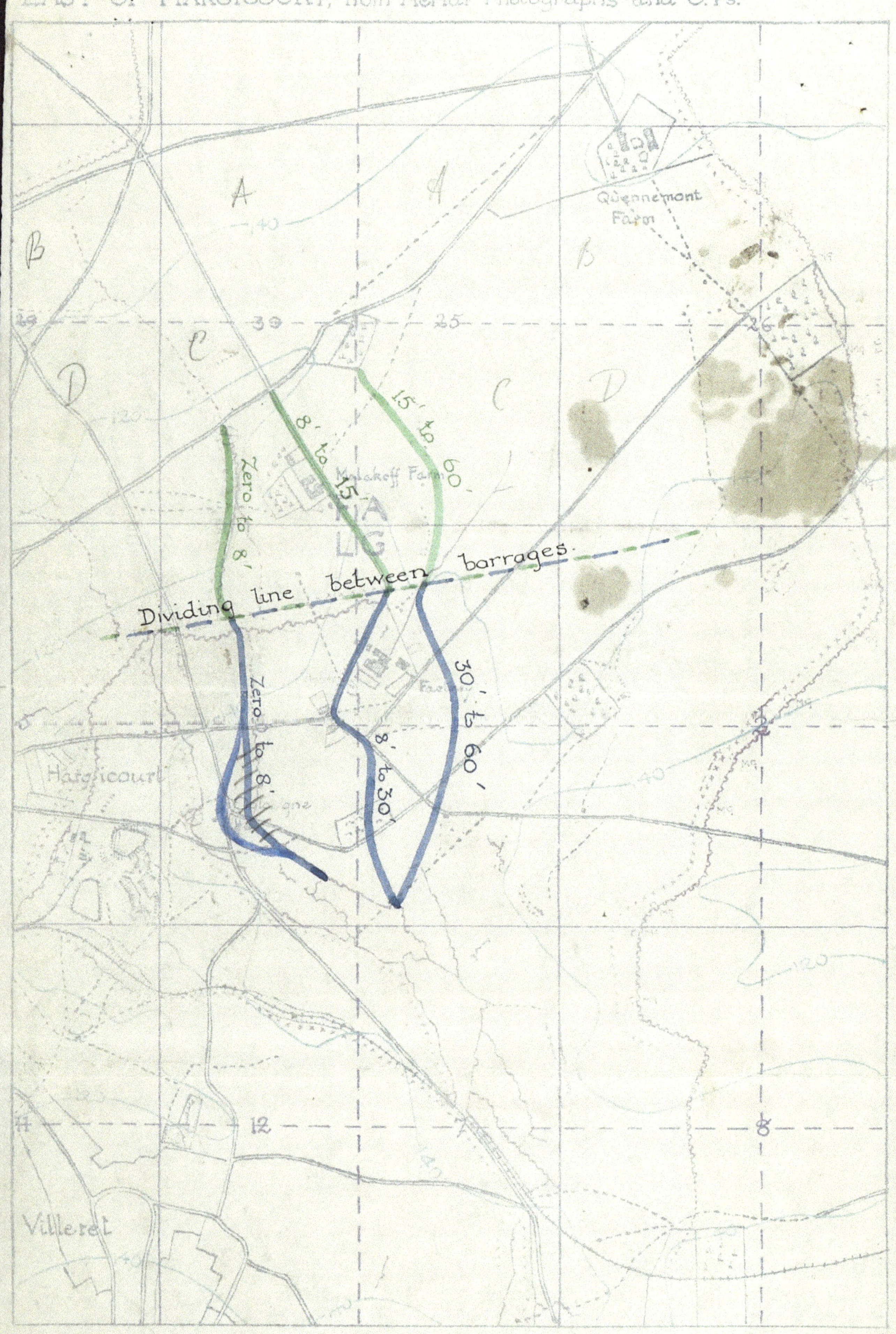
EAST OF HARGICOURT, from Aerial Photographs and O.Ps.
Quennemont Farm
Malakoff Farm
Hargicourt
Villeret
Zero to 8'
8' to 15'
15' to 60'
Dividing line between barrages.
Zero to 8'
8' to 30'
30' to 60'
Scale 1:10,000 Ref. Sheets 62c N.E. & 62b N.W.
Map No 63 1·5·1917
Contours: 20 metres interval.
Trenches Wire Tracks
Suspected M.G. emplacements
Strong Points

Instructions regarding War Diaries and Intelligence Summaries are contained in F. S. Regs., Part II. and the Staff Manual respectively. Title Pages will be prepared in manuscript.

June 1917.

WAR DIARY
~~or~~
~~INTELLIGENCE SUMMARY~~
(Erase heading not required.)

Army Form C. 2118.

2/5th Batt: The Sherwood Foresters.

Vol 5

Place	Date	Hour	Summary of Events and Information	Remarks and references to Appendices
METZ-en-Couture FRANCE.	1917 1st June		Effective strength of battalion on 1st June was, 32 Officers and 698 Other Ranks. The Battalion was in support at METZ-EN-COUTURE (Ref. Map Sheet 57c S.E. – Q.20.), 3 Coys. manning Second line trench and 1 Coy. Intermediate line trench in HAVRINCOURT WOOD. Working parties were found for front line Battalions.	SHW
	5/6 June		Battalion relieved 2/6th Batt: The Sherwood Foresters in front line trenches (Rifle Brigade Sub-Sector); 2 Coys. in front line trenches – Q 11 b 18 to Q 12 a 55; 1 Coy. in support trench in Q 11 d; and 1 Coy. in reserve in Intermediate line trench in Q 17. Coys. were engaged mostly on digging advanced posts and wiring.	SHW
EQUANCOURT	11/12 June		Battalion relieved in front line by 2/5th Batt: North Staffs. Regt. and returned to EQUANCOURT, the 178th Infantry Bde. going into Brigade Reserve in camp at V 16 and V 11. For succeeding 16 days training of all ranks was carried on daily, though a certain number of working parties was found.	SHW

2449 Wt. W14957/M90 750,000 1/16 J.B.C. & A. Forms/C.2118/12.

5.D

Army Form C. 2118.

WAR DIARY ~~or~~ ~~INTELLIGENCE SUMMARY~~

(Erase heading not required.)

Instructions regarding War Diaries and Intelligence Summaries are contained in F. S. Regs., Part II. and the Staff Manual respectively. Title Pages will be prepared in manuscript.

June 1917. 2/5th Batt: The Sherwood Foresters

Place	Date	Hour	Summary of Events and Information	Remarks and references to Appendices
DESSART WOOD (W. 1.)	1917 21 June to 30 June		Battalion relieved 2/4th Batt: lines. Regt in Brigade Reserve at DESSART WOOD (W. 1. b.) Working parties found for front line Battalions by day and night.	Ref. map Sheet 57c S.E. SHW.
			Battle Casualties during month:- NIL. Drafts totalling ~~73~~ 7 Officers and 73 O.R's. arrived during the month	SHW
"	30 June		Effective Strength of Battalion on 30th June:- 39 Officers 741 O.R's.	

G.H. [signature]
Lieut. Col.,
Comdg. 2/5th Batt.
The Sherwood Foresters

2449 Wt. W14957/M90 750,000 1/16 J.B.C. & A. Forms/C.2118/12.

Confidential 2 59

Instructions regarding War Diaries and Intelligence Summaries are contained in F. S. Regs., Part II. and the Staff Manual respectively. Title Pages will be prepared in manuscript.

WAR DIARY
or
~~INTELLIGENCE SUMMARY~~
(Erase heading not required.)

Army Form C. 2118.

2/5th Batt: The Sherwood Foresters

Vol 6

Place	Date	Hour	Summary of Events and Information	Remarks and references to Appendices
VILLERS-PLOUICH	1917 1st July		Batt: relieved 2/6th Batt: The Sherwood Foresters in Front-line trenches E. of VILLERS-PLOUICH from R7a 36 to R7b 82. Batt: H.Q at Q18b98. 2 Coys. in front line and 2 Coys. in support in Sunken Road in Q18b and R13a. Trenches in bad condition when taken over but greatly improved during occupation – front line posts joined up, all trenches widened and deepened and fitted with duckboards; front line wire completed and strengthened. No operations of importance undertaken during tour, and none by enemy on Batt: front.	Ref Map Sheet 57C S.E. JHW
	1917 8th-9th July		On the morning of 8th July, the Commanding Officer Lieut. Col. G.H. ST. HILL was killed by an enemy sniper. He was buried at NEUVILLE-BOURJONVAL (British Cemetery) on 9th July. Major F.E.M. DONNE took over command of the Batt: Batt: relieved evening 8th-9th July by 2 Coys. of 2/5th Batt: The London Regt. and proceeded to camp at EQUANCOURT (V11a.) to rest for a few hours, thence marching on 9th to Training Area in O.35.	JHW Ref Map Sheet 57c S.W. JHW

2449 Wt. W14957/M90 750,000 1/16 J.B.C. & A. Forms/C.2118/12.

Confidential

Instructions regarding War Diaries and Intelligence Summaries are contained in F. S. Regs., Part II. and the Staff Manual respectively. Title Pages will be prepared in manuscript.

WAR DIARY

~~or~~

~~INTELLIGENCE~~ ~~SUMMARY~~

(Erase heading not required.)

Army Form C. 2118.

2/5th Sherwood Foresters

Place	Date	Hour	Summary of Events and Information	Remarks and references to Appendices
O. 35 (Sheet 57c SE)	1917. 9th - 31st July		Training carried out daily under Divisional Programme. Frequent Brigade and Divisional Tactical Exercises in Trench to Trench Attack, etc. All Coys. fired on 30x Range (Grouping, application & rapid practices). All Coys. carried out Field Firing.	SHW.
			All Companies re-inoculated during this period.	
	14th July		Major F.E.M. DONNE appointed IV Corps Burial Officer. CAPT T.H.L. STEBBING took over command of Batt:	SHW
	28th July		LT-COL. H. R. GADD, M.C. assumed command of the Batt: on this date.	SHW.
			Effective Strength of Batt on 1st July 1917:- Officers 38 - O.R. 735	
			" " " 31st July 1917:- do. 38 - " 721	
			Battle Casualties Killed 2, Wounded 10.	

H.R. Gadd Lieut. Col.
Comdg. 2/5th Batt: The Sherwood Foresters

2449 Wt. W14957/M90 750,000 1/16 J.B.C. & A. Forms/C.2118/12.

Confidential

Instructions regarding War Diaries and Intelligence Summaries are contained in F. S. Regs., Part II. and the Staff Manual respectively. Title Pages will be prepared in manuscript.

WAR DIARY
or
~~INTELLIGENCE~~ SUMMARY
(Erase heading not required.)

Army Form C. 2118.

2/5th Batt: The Sherwood Foresters

Place	Date	Hour	Summary of Events and Information	Remarks and references to Appendices
LE MESNIL-EN-ARROUAISE FRANCE Sheet 57c O.35.d.	1917 AUG 1-24th		Effective Strength of Batt: on 1st Aug:- Officers 39, Other Ranks 716.	
			Battalion in camp at O.35.d. Divisional Training in accordance with S.S. 135 carried out. Brigade and Divisional Field Days, and Night Operations. Platoon Training. All Coys. put through short Bombing Course and every man threw a live Bomb. Field Firing Practice and Musketry on 30x Range. Special training of Specialists – Scouts, Snipers, Runners, Lewis Gunners etc. Trench Raids practised.	JRN [?]
	AUG 5th		Draft of 53 N.C.O's and men arrived	
	15th		Draft of 179 N.C.O's and men arrived.	
	AUG 24th		Battalion moved to BRUCE HUTS, AVELUY. (Ref Map ALBERT (Combined Sheet) 1/40000) W.16.a. First half of journey on Motor Buses – second half by Route March.	

Confidential

Instructions regarding War Diaries and Intelligence Summaries are contained in F. S. Regs., Part II. and the Staff Manual respectively. Title Pages will be prepared in manuscript.

WAR DIARY
or
~~INTELLIGENCE~~ SUMMARY

(Erase heading not required.)

Army Form C. 2118.

2/5th Batt The Sherwood Foresters

Place	Date	Hour	Summary of Events and Information	Remarks and references to Appendices
BRUCE HUTS AVELUY (ALBERT Combined Sheet 1/40000) W.16a	1917 AUG 26th – 31st		Training continued. Modifications in form of attack practised.	S.H.W.
	AUG 31		Effective Strength of Batt on 31st Aug: Officers 37, Other Ranks 955	S.H.W.

H.H. Reed [signature] Lieut. Col
Comdg. 2/5th Batt
The Sherwood Foresters.

2449 Wt. W14957/M90 750,000 1/16 J.B.C. & A. Forms/C.2118/12.

Confidential

Instructions regarding War Diaries and Intelligence Summaries are contained in F. S. Regs., Part II. and the Staff Manual respectively. Title Pages will be prepared in manuscript.

WAR DIARY
~~or~~
~~INTELLIGENCE~~ SUMMARY

(Erase heading not required.)

Army Form C. 2118.

2/5th Sherwood Foresters.

128/5·9 Vol 8.

Place	Date	Hour	Summary of Events and Information	Remarks and references to Appendices
France. Ref. Map. Sheet 27. J. 2. a 80.	1917 ~~Sept 1~~ Aug. 31		(Ref. Map ALBERT 40000) The Batt: left AVELUY by Route March at 3.25 a.m. on 31st August. Entrained at BEAUCOURT at 5.30 a.m. together with Transport and detrained at GODESVAERVELDE at 4 p.m. Thence the Batt: marched via STEENVOORDE and WINNIZEELE to camp at J.2 a 80 arriving at 11.30 p.m. No casualties.	J.H.W.
	Sept 1st		Effective Strength of Batt: on this date :- Officers 36, O. Rs. 949.	J.H.W.
	2nd		Sunday. Usual Divine Services.	J.H.W.
	3rd		Training by Companies. Close Order Drill and Attack practice.	J.H.W.
	4th		Brigade Tactical Exercise.	J.H.W.
	5th		Batt: Tactical Exercise in afternoon. Bathing in morning.	J.H.W.
	6th		Close Order Drill and Attack Practice by Companies on ground near Camp.	J.H.W.
	7th		Batt: Tactical Exercise on B'de. Training ground at ST. ACAIRE.	J.H.W.
	8th		Brigade Tactical Exercise. "	J.H.W.
	9th		Sunday. Divine Services and Bathing.	J.H.W.
	10th		Companies at Disposal of Coy. Comdrs for Battle training. Short Route March in afternoon.	J.H.W.
	11th		Brigade Route March of about 12 miles.	J.H.W.

2/5 Notts & Derby ... (illegible marginal note)

2449 Wt. W14957/M90 750,000 1/16 J.B.C. & A. Forms/C.2118/12.

Confidential

Instructions regarding War Diaries and Intelligence Summaries are contained in F. S. Regs., Part II. and the Staff Manual respectively. Title Pages will be prepared in manuscript.

WAR DIARY
or
~~INTELLIGENCE SUMMARY~~
(Erase heading not required.)

Army Form C. 2118.

2/5 Sherwood Foresters.

Place	Date	Hour	Summary of Events and Information	Remarks and references to Appendices
FRANCE Ref. Map Sheet 27 J2a80.	1917 Sep. 12		Coys. at Close Order and Battle Drill. Bathing in morning.	SHW
	" 13		Coys. at disposal of Coy. Comdrs. during morning for YUKON PACK practice, Musketry, and Gas Drill. Infty Operations. Practice Relief of Units holding a line of Shell Holes	SHW
	" 14th		Battalion Drill. Musketry. Gas Drill and Rifle Grenade practice.	SHW
	" 15th		Musketry - Phys. Training - Patrolling - YUKON PACK competition. Bathing.	SHW
	16th		11 Officers and 450 O.R's proceeded to TILQUES area for a 3 days' Course of Musketry at V. Army School of Musketry. Details left in camp under command of Major R C TRENCH	SHW
	17th		Details of Coys. (Organised as Platoons of Composite Coy.) took part in Bde. Tactical Exercise under orders of O.C. 2/7th Batt.	SHW
	18th		Musketry. L.G. training. Bayonet Fighting. Gas Drill & Phys. Training	SHW
	19th		Close Order Drill, etc. Musketry party returned from V. Army School.	SHW
	20th		Batt: moved by route march to camp at L.8 c 35 leaving camp at 5.55 am.	SHW

Confidential

Instructions regarding War Diaries and Intelligence Summaries are contained in F. S. Regs., Part II. and the Staff Manual respectively. Title Pages will be prepared in manuscript.

WAR DIARY

~~or~~

~~INTELLIGENCE SUMMARY~~

(Erase heading not required.)

Army Form C. 2118.

2/5th Batt: Sherwood Foresters

Place	Date	Hour	Summary of Events and Information	Remarks and references to Appendices
FRANCE Ref. Map Sheet 27 - L 8 c 35	1917. 21st Sep		Work in Camp.	JHW
	22nd "		Close Order Drill. Gas Drill. Phys. training & B. F., Kit Inspections, etc	JHW
	23rd		Sunday. Divine Services. Batt: moved by Route March to Camp at G 6 d 44 (Sheet 28 1/40000). Batt. moved off at 3.35 pm. and marched by SWITCH ROAD, N. of POPERINGHE, - main POPERINGHE - VLAMERTINGHE ROAD to Destination, "B" Camp.	JHW
	~~24th~~		~~Coys. at disposal of Coy. Comdrs. for completion of fighting order Kit, and making of all preliminary arrangements for moving up into line.~~	~~JHW~~

2449 Wt. W14957/M90 750,000 1/16 J.B.C. & A. Forms/C.2118/12.

Confidential

Instructions regarding War Diaries and Intelligence Summaries are contained in F. S. Regs., Part II. and the Staff Manual respectively. Title Pages will be prepared in manuscript.

WAR DIARY
or
~~INTELLIGENCE SUMMARY~~
(Erase heading not required.)

Army Form C. 2118.

2/5 Battn. The Sherwood Foresters.

Place	Date 1917	Hour	Summary of Events and Information	Remarks and references to Appendices
Sheet 28 NW Belgium G 6 d 4 4.	Sep. 24		The day was spent in equipping the men of the Battn. with all articles carried in fighting kit.	
		6 pm.	The Battn (less those left behind) moved to CALL RESERVE @ C 23 c 8.6 under Major Trench, arriving at 11.5 pm and relieved 2/6 NORTH STAFFS. Relief completed by 12.10 am	See O.O. 22. JA
	25.	6. pm	Final preparations for attack. C.O. held several conferences with O.C Coys. TRIAL Barrage.	
		11.30 pm	B & C Coys. moved into position on tape	See OO 21. Inst. No 4. JA
		12 md.	A & D Coys moved into position on tape.	
	26.		ZERO DAY.	
		2.10 am	Companies reported in position ready for attack.	
		3.50 am	Commencement of Bombardment of 2 hrs. duration previous to ZERO HOUR. (Enemy retaliation Barrage on his Barrage Lines.)	
		5.50 am	ZERO HOUR. For report on operations see description attached.	
		10.15 am	Btn. Head Qrs. move from Capricorn KEEP to GALLIPOLI.	
		6 pm.	Commencement of Retrograde Movement. (see description attached)	JA
	27.		Battn hold front line	
		6.40. am	S.O.S. asked for from front line	
		6.5? pm	S.O.S. asked for again owing to counter-attack.	JA
	28	5.45 am	Our barrage came down in front of FRONT LINE and reported as falling short in places.	
		6.15 am	Low-flying enemy aeroplane passed over our lines and appeared to signal by means of smoke bombs.	
		6 pm	Bn. H.Qrs left GALLIPOLI and reopened at CAPRICORN KEEP at 6.15 pm. Relieved by 2/6 Sherwood Foresters and Battn. kept in SUPPORT. Relief complete 2.15 am. and Brigade advised.	JA

2449 Wt. W14957/M90 750,000 1/16 J.B.C. & A. Forms/C.2118/12.

Confidential

Instructions regarding War Diaries and Intelligence Summaries are contained in F. S. Regs., Part II. and the Staff Manual respectively. Title Pages will be prepared in manuscript.

WAR DIARY
or
~~INTELLIGENCE SUMMARY~~
(Erase heading not required.)

2/5th Battn. The Sherwood Foresters.

Army Form C. 2118.

Place	Date 1917	Hour	Summary of Events and Information	Remarks and references to Appendices
	Sep. 29.	2-3 am	Gas shelling by enemy.	
		5.20 am	Barrage came down on CAPRICORN in response to ours.	
		9.30 am	C.O. interviewed Officers of Relieving Battn.	
		4 pm	Operation Orders issued for relief.	O.O. No 23
			Battn relieved by 2 platoons of CANTERBURY BATTN. and proceeded to VLAMERTINGHE No 2 AREA arriving at approx 10 p.m.	
		10.45 pm	Enemy planes drop bombs on camp and injure several horses in Transport Lines.	JH
	30.		Battn. spent time in cleaning up, checking rolls, making up casualty returns. Enemy aeroplanes again drop bombs on & around camp ground.	JH

2449 Wt. W14957/M90 750,000 1/16 J.B.C. & A. Forms/C.2118/12.

MAP A

1:10 000 K.3. EDITION I. Parts of { 28 N.E. 28 N.W.

FIELD SURVEY COY. R.E. (2581) 16-9-17

Scale. 1:10,000.

YARDS 500 400 300 200 100 0 500 1,000 YARDS

VARIATION 12° 23'

Message Form.

....................Division.

Map reference or mark own position on Map at back.

1. I am at...

2. I am at...and am consolidating.

3. I am at...and have consolidated.

4. I need:—Ammunition.
   Bombs.
   Rifle Grenades.
   Water.
   Very lights.
   Stokes shells.

5. Enemy forming up for counter-attack at...... ....

6. I am in touch with.................................. on Right/Left at ....

7. I am not in touch on Right/Left

8. Am being shelled from...

9. I estimate my present strength at ....rifles.

10. Hostile {Battery / Machine Gun / Trench Mortar} active at..

Time.................................a.m. (p.m.)

Name...

Date...

Platoon.................. Company...........

Place..

Battalion...

OPERATION ORDER NO. 22
by
LIEUT.COL. H.R. GADD, M.C.
Commanding 2/5th Sherwood Foresters 24 Sept. 1917.

1. Ref para. 2 Operation Order No. 21.

2. The Batt. will parade in Mass today by "A" and "B" Coys. lines in time to move off by 6 p.m. and will proceed by following route :- VLAMERTINGH I. 7 c 89 - SALVATION CORNER - I. 2 c33 - No. 6 Track to Destination in "B" A rea in C. 23 c.

3. Guides will meet the Battalion at C. 22 d.72 at 10 p.m.

4. Guides will be provided as follows:-
1 Batt. H.Q.
1 for each Coy. H.Q.
1 for R.A. P.
1 for each Platoon.
6.

5. Guides have received instructions to conduct O.C.Platoons to Coy. H.Q. after thePlatoons have been placed in position. O.C. Coys. will report to Batt. H.Q. when move is complete.

6. Batt. H.Q. will be about C.23c76.

7. 2 Limber Waggons per Coy. and 1 Limber Waggon for H.Q.Coy will be available for taking up rations tools Lewis Guns etc.. These waggons and the M.O.'s cart will be accom anied by Coy. Q.M.S,'s and will be at C.28b5570 at 1 a.m. tomorow. M.O. and O.C.Coys. will arrange to draw at that hour. Limber waggons will then return to new camp.

8. Intervals. The following intervals will be kept. From Camp, 300 yds between Coys. E. of VLAMERTINGHE, 200 yds. between Platoons.

9. No transport is allowed E. of VLAMERTINGHE before 9.40 p.m.

10. Limber waggons will report to Coys. at 4 p,m. The M.O.'s Cart will be by Medical Inspection Hut at same time.

11. Greatcoats will be dumped at Q.M.'s Stores by 5 p.m.

(Sd.) F.E.ANDREWS,
2/Lt. & A/Adjt.

OPERATION ORDERS NO. 21
by
Lieut. Col. H.R. GADD, M.C., Comg.
2/6th Batt. Sherwood Foresters.

INSTRUCTIONS NO. 4 25th Sept. 1917.

Map Ref. GRAVENSTAFEL 1/10000

1. The Batt. will assemble in attack formation on the line of emplacements D.13c19.
B & D. Coys. will proceed by WIELTJE - GRAVENSTAFEL Road and C & A Coys. by No. 5 Track. Coys will leave their present positions as under:-
B & C Coys. 11.30 p.m.
A & D Coys. 12 midnight.
All Coys. will be in position by 2.30 a.m.
As soon as the Coys. are in position a runner will be sent to Batt. H.Q.
As soon as a Coy. is in position all tapes will be taken up.
Coys. wi ll mark out their assembly lines in accordance with verbal instructions issued by the C.O.

2. Watches will be synchronised at Batt. H.Q. at 7 p.m. and 9 p.m. tonight The same Officer will attend in each case.

3. Ref. Instructions No. 3 para. 4 line 8 for Zero plus 1 hour 40 mins. read " Between Zero plus 1 hour 2 mins. and Zero plus 1 hour 40 mins Batt. goes through 2/5th Sherwood Foresters and at Zero plus 1 hour 40 mins. the barrage commences to creep again. The barrage will lift off OTTO ROAD at Zero plus 3 hours 11 mins.".

4 All Stores not being carried by the Batt. in the Assault will be dumped present Batt. H.Q. Cpl. Presss will be in charge and will receive further orders ~~after~~ as to sending u p the stores.

5. Rations will be delivered tonight at 8 p.m.

6. Batt. H.Q. will be at C.18d86 and will move after the final objective has been captured to about D 14 c49.
(Note that this position is different to that given in verbal instructions).

7. The R.A.P. will be at CAPRICORN KEEP until the capture of the final objective when it will move forward to KEIR FARM.

8. The Bde. Dump is at C.18d98. It contains S.A.A., Bombs, Vey Lights, Ground Flares , and rserve Rations. Petrol tins of water are situated at C.18 d 98 and C 28 b 37. Units drawing water from either of these two places will leave an empty petrol tim for every full one drawn. No water will be drawn before 9 a.m.tomorrow.

(Sd.) E.E. ANDREWS,
2/Lt. & A/ADJT.

2/5th Battalion The Sherwood Foresters.

SECRET.

Report on Operations 26th September 1917.

1. GENERAL On the morning of 26th inst, the Battalion under my Command attacked the enemy's position, in conjunction with the troops of 178th Infantry Brigade, and in accordance with the orders received from the Brig Genl, 178th Infantry Brigade. The role allotted to the Battalion was to support 2/8th S,F. until their second objective had been reached and then to pass through them and capture and consolidate the line of the enclosure D. 14.b.4.4. - D.14.d.7.7.

OTTO FARM was then to becaptured and held, and a line of posts was to be established on this general line.

2. DISPOSITIONS

My dispositions were regulated by verbal instructions received from B.G.C. 178th Infantry Brigade, which entaled keeping one Company as a reserve in its forming up place and sending only two platoons forward to OTTO FARM.

I had previously determined that it would require two Companies to attack and hold OTTO FARM, but my plans had to be modified in accordance with the above.

B. Company therefore was ordered to attack the enclosure D. 14.b.4.4. and C Company to reach this line and when the barrage lifted off OTTO to attack it and hold it with two platoons, leaving the third to holdthe line to B Coys right.

D Company detailed one platoon to mop up for B and C Coys and the remainder were detailed as an immediate support to the two attacking Companies.

A Company was retained as a general reserve about AISNE FARM.

3. APPRECIATION.

As OTTO FARM was to be held I considered it important to ensur that the 177th Infantry Brigade on my right were fully cognisant of thefact and were prepared to establish a line of posts to protect its right flank.

On the afternoon of the 25th instant, I therefore sent my Adjutant to the 2/5th Lincs Regt to explain my plan and to impress the above point on them. He did not consider that the arrangements thay had already made were sufficient for our support and informed 178th Inf: Bde H.Q. of the fact.

The two Brigades concerned then succeeded in co-ordinating a schemewhich would ensure satisfactory mutual support between the Bwo Battalions.

4.ASSEMBLY LINES. Assembly positions were marked out in accordance with Brigade Instructions, the front line of deploymet being our line of emplacements D.13.c.2.6. and my left being on the road. The depth of he Battalion was about 300 yards. D Company formed up behind B Coy on left and A Company behind C Coy on right.

At 4 a.m. in reply to our preliminary bombardment, the enemy put down a heavy barrage and D and A Compamy suffered considerable casualties.

5. THE ASSAULT At 5.30 a.m. the assault commencd and a general advance was begun. From the outset the Battalion experienced great difficulties in maitnaing direction. The WIELTJE - GRAVENSTAFEL Road was vey difficult to determine and compases proved unreliable. The Battalion, however, succeeded in passing through 2/6th S.F. to time and continued the attack. Very little opposition was encoune-tered by my two attacking Coys but the greatest difficulty was still experienced in keeping organization and direction.

The thick fog and the dust and smoke giving the attackers all the difficulties of a night advance. The enclosure was captured by B Company, and Capt Littleboy, Commanding C Company collected his men preparatory to assaulting OTTO FARM. As the twp platoons detailed for this purpose appeared too weak, Capt Littleboy collected all the men of his Coy available.

6.CAPTURE OF OTTO FARM. The Company advanced and got as close to the Barrage as possible when it lifted the assault was delivered. A certain amount of opposition was encountered, but the place was bombed and most of the garrison ran out. Many were killed and about 40 prisoners were taken.

Touch was made with 177th Inf Bde on right.

7.POSITION AFTER THE ASSAULT. at 10 a.m. my situation was shewn on attached Map A. Captain Swan and the remains of B Company were holding the enclosure and had pushed out a line of posts connecting it with OTTO FARM, and OTTO FARM was held by about 15 men of C Company. The remainder of these two Companies were either casualties or had lost their way and were not available for reserves. The whole of B Company had suffered very heavy and casualties from shell fire and all their officers had been wounded (N.B. this Company at the end of the day only numbered 28). Of these that were left, some had joined Capt. Swan in theenclosure and others, Capt Littleboy in OTTO FARM. I therefore deemed it necessary to moveforward to DEEP TRENCH D.14.d.1.9. This they had to do through a heavy barrage and as they had sustained heavy casualties before ZERO their fighting efficiency on arrival was very small.

8. WITHDRAWAL FROM OTTO FARM. Meanwhile Capt Littleboy had personally been to see an officer of the 2/5th Lincolns on his right and had arr arranged with him for the protetion of his right flank. Shortly after this the enemy opened fire on thetroops on his right, and they appeared to suffer heavily. They then withdrew about 500 yards leaving his right flank uncovered. A defensive flank was then formed with a Lewis Gun and Capt. Littleboy again went to the Battalion on his right and asked an officer why they had retired. He pointed out that OTTO FARM was beyond their objective and he did notpropose to hold that forward line. Early in the afternoon a small local counter- attack on OTTO FARM was repulsed by riflefire from the farm. About 5 o'clock the enemy opened a heavy barrage along the front, and particularly against the 177th Brigade on the right and the counter attack was seen developing from N.E. DOCHY FARM. Theretrograde movement of our troops in various parts could then be seen in progress and Captain Littleboy in OTTO FARM could see the enemy to his right rear threatening B Company in the enclosure and the line further to the left. With the objetive of preventing the apparent rolling up of the line thetroops from OTTO FARM were withdrawn by him and the line of B Company was prolonged and covered to the right. Just before it was dark, many of the troops who had retired returned, and the line was firmly established on the line of the enclosure.

9. SUBSEQUENT PROCEEDINGS Little could be done in the way of re-organization during the night 26/27th as the situation was for a long time very obscure and it was considered more important for the troo of the Battalion, all of which were in thefront line, to maintaine the positions they were in. Further German counter attackes were expected (N.B. the strength of the Battalion holding this line at present was 171). During the night stragglers were collected and a reserve of about 30 men was made near Gallipoli to which Battalion Headquartes had moved. About 4 a.m. on the morning of the 27th, as soon as it was practical to do so, this reerve was ordered forward to about DEEP TRENCH, but as they were starting a very heavy hostile barrage was put down and their move was postponed until daylight, when it was cancelld. On thenight of the 28/29th the Battalion was relieved by the 2/6th S.F. and was reformed about GALLIPOLI where it remained in support of the 2/6th.

10. GENERAL All ranks displayed at all times an offensive and soldier likespirit and the men reponded to every call made upon them. A number lost their way during the attack, but in practically every case I am satisfied they joined up as soon as possible. During the retirement during the evening of the 26th some joined in, but the greater portion of them only retred on to the supporting troops two or three hundred yards in rear and soon came forward to rejoin their comrades.

15 of them reached WIELTJE and were returned on the following morning and a few were collected by me in the neighbourhood of GALLIPOLI.

I am in possession of the namesof most of those who went pastxBatax Battalion Headquarters and enquiry is being held into their conduct.

11. HONOURS AND AWARDS The names of all those particularly deserving of award are being forwarded under separate cover.

12. POINTS FOR CONSIDERATION. In accordance with 178th Infantry Brigade 688 G. of the 1st October, I beg to bring forward the following points:-

(1) It was very difficult to find the final objective and to keep direction as stated in the above report.

(2) The Barrage was very suitable and troops could get within 50 yads of it. They however, continually got mixed up in it.

(3) Formations were suitable. It was found vry hard to keep these formations owing to fog and smoke.
They are however considered the most suitable.

(4) The dress and equipment was satisfactory in every way excepting that bombs should be carried in the side pockets.

(5) Owing to the confusion during the first night, little could bed done for thecomfort of the assaulting troops.

(6) This was not satisfactory. Tapes should be put out at least the night before, and the C.O. and Company Commanders given a chance of inspecting them. It would also be very useful if a map could be supplied shewing 4 exact lines of enemy's barrage. It requires watching carefully for at le least three days previous to the attack. This can only be done satisfactorily by people living in the line.

(7) For the front line shell holes improved to shoot out of appear to be the best. No casualties were incurred by the the Battalion after the termination of the fighting in the front line composed of shell holes, although it was heavily bombarded several times.

(8) If machine xxx xxxxxxxxx guns are allotted to Battalions they must join them in time to march to the position of assembly.

Map 'A' Attached

(Sgd) H R Gadd

Lieutenant Colonel.

Commanding 2/5th Battn, The Sherwood Foresters.

OPERATION ORDER NO. 23
by
Lieut. Col H.R. GADD, M.C., Comg.
2/5 th Battalion, Sherwood Foresters. 29. 9. 17.

1. The Batt. will be relieved by 2 Platoons of 2nd. ~~3~~ Canterbury Batt. and on relief will proceed to No. 2 Area VLAMERTINGHE.

2. Only "B" Coy. will be relieved.
At 7.30 p.m. A & C Coys. will move off and B Coy. will wait until it is relieved. D Coy. will follow B Coy.

3. Guides, B Coy. 2 and 1 for R.A.P. will be at SPREE FARM by 7.p.m. tonight.

4. Route will be :-
Batt. H.Q. - WIELTJE - ST. JEAN - WALL CROSS RDS - SALVATION CORNER - VLAMERTINGHE. Movement until W. of YPRES by parties of about 15 men at 100 yds. interval, when clear of YPRES will collect and march to VLAMERTINGHE independently.

5. Guides will be at Cross Roads E. of VLAMERTINGHE at 1 a.m.

6. As each Coy. comes past Batt. H.Q. the Coy. Comdr. will report com letion of relief.

7. One Waggon per Coy. and 1 for H.Q. and Medical Cart will be at C23c21 (Junction of CALL RESERVE and Road) by 9 p.m. All Kit for these waggons will be left at this spot as Coys. march past A small party left behind will be in charge. Coys. will hand over all tools, maps, and aeroplane photos. etc. also all Very Lights, S.O.S., and boxes of S.A.A. Lists of these stores will be made out and a receipt obtained and forwarded to the Adjutant. Coys. will make every endeavour to come out of the line complete in Coy. Stores. All full petrol tins will be handed over and empty ones dumped at Bde. H.Q;

8. Acknowledge.

(Sd) F.E.Andrews,

2/Lt. & A/Adjt.

Issued at 3.30 p.m.

Confidential

Instructions regarding War Diaries and Intelligence Summaries are contained in F. S. Regs., Part II. and the Staff Manual respectively. Title Pages will be prepared in manuscript.

WAR DIARY
or
~~INTELLIGENCE SUMMARY~~
(Erase heading not required.)

Army Form C. 2118.

2/5th Batt: The Sherwood Foresters.

Vol 9

Place	Date 1917	Hour	Summary of Events and Information	Remarks and references to Appendices
	Octr. 1	8.30 am	Battn left VLAMERTINGHE by train for STEENBECQUE (arrived 12.30 pm) and marched to billets at LES CISEAUX. Effective Strength 26 Officers 666 ORs.	OO No 24 F.L.S.
LES CISEAUX	2	9.30 am	Visit of Brigadier to the Battn. Clothing Board held, & inspection of Lewis Guns held. Description of Battalion's Operations on the 26th Septr. written by C.O.	F.L.S. See copy attd Sep 26th 1917.
	3	10 am	C.O. attended conference of Brigadiers and Battn. Commanders at Divisional Head Quarters at STEENBECQUE	F.L.S.
		3 pm	Inspection by G.O.C of 178th Brigade at Brigade Head Quarters BOESEGHEM. During the day the Battn. did P.T and Close order drill.	F.L.S.
	4	9.30 am	Divine Service with Brigade Band in attendance. Battn under command of Major Trench P.T. and Close Order Drill parades held.	F.L.S.
	5	9.30 am	Battn left LES CISEAUX in Busses for THEROUANNE STATION where they debussed and then marched to DELETTE arriving at 2.15 pm.	O.O. No 25. F.L.S.
DELETTE	6	2.15 pm	Training of L. Gunners & Rifle Grenadiers carried out under shelter owing to weather. Inspection of draft by Commanding Officer.	F.L.S.
	7		Usual divine Services.	F.L.S.

2449 Wt. W14957/M90 750,000 1/16 J.B.C. & A. Forms/C.2118/12.

Confidential

Instructions regarding War Diaries and Intelligence Summaries are contained in F. S. Regs., Part II. and the Staff Manual respectively. Title Pages will be prepared in manuscript.

WAR DIARY
or
~~INTELLIGENCE~~ SUMMARY
(Erase heading not required.)

2/5 Battn The Sherwood Foresters.

Army Form C. 2118.

Place	Date	Hour	Summary of Events and Information	Remarks and references to Appendices
DELETTE	8.10.17		Battn training under Platoon arrangements. 1 Hours Company drill during morning. "A" Coy inspected by Commanding Officer. Draft inspected by Brigadier at 12.30 pm.	F.L.S.
	9.10.17		Battn training under Platoon arrangements. 1 Hours Company drill from 9.30 am to 10.30 am. "B" Coy inspected by Commanding Officer.	F.L.S.
	10.10.17		Battn. moved from DELETTE to BAILLEUL-les-PERNES and AUMERVAL. Left at 11 am and arrived at destination at 5.30 pm.	O.O. No 27
	11.10.17		Battn. moved from BAILLEUL-les-Pernes and AUMERVAL at 9 Am to CAMBLAIN-CHÂTELAIN. Arrived at 10.20 am. but had to wait until 11.30 am before occupying billets owing to 2/5 LINCOLNS not having left.	O.O. No 28
	12.10.17		BATTN. moved from CAMBLAIN-CHÂTELAIN to COUPIGNY. Left at 9.45 am and arrived at 3.30 pm.	O.O. No 29
	13.10.17		Battn moved from COUPIGNY to GOUY-SERVINS. Left at 11. am and arrived at 12.45 pm.	O.O. No 30
GOUY-SERVINS	14.10.17		Usual divine services at 9.30 am. Inspections of Kit and boots held during day.	
	15.10.17		Working Party of 200 sent under 4 officers to SOUCHEZ. The remainder of Battn did Close order Drill, PT & BF during day.	
	16.10.17		Battalion bathed at CARENCY (100 at a time) commencing at 9. am. PT & BF done to fill up time before and after bathing.	

2449 Wt. W14957/M90 750,000 1/16 J.B.C. & A. Forms/C.2118/12.

Confidential.

Instructions regarding War Diaries and Intelligence Summaries are contained in F. S. Regs., Part II. and the Staff Manual respectively. Title Pages will be prepared in manuscript.

WAR DIARY
or
INTELLIGENCE SUMMARY

(Erase heading not required.)

2/5 BATTN. The Sherwood Foresters

Army Form C. 2118.

Place	Date	Hour	Summary of Events and Information	Remarks and references to Appendices
GOUY-SERVINS	Oct. 1917 17		Working Party of 200 sent to SOUCHEZ under 4 officers. 50% of remaining NCOs & officers attended demonstration at LENS JUNCTION in "Revetting".	E.L.S.
	18.		C.O. Adj. 2nd in Command and all Company Commanders visited line near AVION and made arrangements re Relief. Battn. practised in BF & PT Coy Drill and Squad Drill.	E.L.S.
	19.		Working Party of 200 Sent to SOUCHEZ. Remainder training under Coy arrangements.	E.L.S.
	20.		Preparations for moving into AVION sector of line. Coy Commanders and 7 OR. left GOUY-SERVINS at 4pm for line.	E.L.S.
	21.		Battn relieved The Leicester Regiment in Avion Sector near LENS from N.33.d.4.4. to N32.b.9.6 (QUEBEC RD MAP) leaving GOUY-SERVINS at 5.0 PM and travelling by decauville railway as far as LA COULOTTE.	OO No 31 E.L.S.
	22.		Day quiet. AVION TRENCH Shelled at about 10.30 AM. Two casualties.	E.L.S.
	23.		Day quiet.	E.L.S.
	24.		AVION TRENCH right of CYRIL TRENCH badly shelled by 4.2's during morning and almost obliterated. Trench cleared after dark.	E.L.S.
	25.		Day quiet. At 11.0 PM gas drums were successfully projected from position behind our front line. No retaliation and no rockets sent up.	O.O. No. 35. E.L.S.
	26.		Day quiet. Draft of 62 O.R. arrived from 12th Battn. S.F. and were accomodated in support trenches. (RED TRENCH)	

2449 Wt. W14957/M90 750,000 1/16 J.B.C. & A. Forms/C.2118/12.

Army Form C. 2118.

Instructions regarding War Diaries and Intelligence Summaries are contained in F. S. Regs., Part II. and the Staff Manual respectively. Title Pages will be prepared in manuscript.

WAR DIARY or INTELLIGENCE SUMMARY

(Erase heading not required.)

2/5th BATTN. The Sherwood Foresters.

Place	Date	Hour	Summary of Events and Information	Remarks and references to Appendices
	Oct. 27th		Battn. Hdqrs. moved to position lately occupied by R.A.P.	O.O. No 36
	28th		Heavy shelling of Battn. Hdqrs. by 4.2's from 9.0 AM to 11.30 AM.	
	29th		Day quiet. Battn. relieved by 2/7th Sherwood Foresters and proceeded to support line (RED TRENCH)	O.O. No.
	30th		Day quiet. Trench wardens and working parties found by coys.	
	31st		Day quiet. Working parties etc same as for 30th. 1 Casualty. / Effective Strength 38 Officers 767 Other Ranks	

[signature] Lieut Col
Comdg 2/5th Sherwood Foresters

2449 Wt. W14957/M90 750,000 1/16 J.B.C. & A. Forms/C.2118/12.

To :-   OPERATION   ORDERS   No. 24

by

Lt. Col. H.R. GADD.   M.C.,

Commanding

2/5th. Battal ion, The Sherwood Foresters.

1.10.1917.

ADMINISTRATIVE   INSTRUCTIONS   No. 1 .

Reference Maps 1/40,000 Sheet 28
1/100,000 Sheet 5 a.

1. Paras. 1,2,3,4,6,9 and 10 of Warning Orders No. 1 hold good.

2. The Battalion will entrain at VLAMERTINGHE STATION, and detrain at STEENBECQUE. It will parade ready to move off at 6.45 a.m. Details at Transport Lines will be marched to Camp by 6.30 a.m. They will have breakfast at Transport Lines before being marched over.

3. The 4 Cookers, 2 Water Carts, Mess Cart and Maltese Cart will proceed on train leaving VLAMERTINGHE STATION at 3.5. p.m. The MessCart and Maltese Cart will be at camp by 6.0 a.m. The Transport Officer will accompany this portion, and is responsible that it is at entraining station by 1.5 p.m.

4. Reference para. 5 of Warning Order, blankets will be dumped at Guard Tent by 5.30 a.m., and loaded on baggage wagons by party detailed. The wagon will leave camp by 6 a.m. The Transport Officer will ensure that this wagon joins the remainder of Transport proceeding by road at Brigade Transport Lines in good time.

5. Lewis Guns will be loaded on Limbers by 6 a.m.

6. Reference para. 3 of Warning Order the loading party will proceed with transport which entrains in afternoon.

7. Reveille 4.30 a.m.   Breakfast 5.30 a.m.

8. Acknowledge.

G.H. WILLIAMSON,
Lieutenant and Adjutant,
2/5th. Battalion, The Sherwood Foresters

Issued at 2.45 a.m. to all recipients of
WARNING ORDERS No. 1

OPERATION ORDER. No.25.

by

LIEUTENANT COLONEL.H.R.GADD.M.C.

Commanding 2/5th Battalion. The Sherwood Foresters.

4th Octr.1917.

Reference Map.HAZEBROUCK Sheet.5.a.

1. The Battalion will move tomorrow by bus and route march to DELETTE.

2. "Embussing point" - Cross roads N. of third E in BOESEGHEM.
Time 9.30.a.m.
Debussing point:- Road junction N of "A" in STA which is S.E. of THEROUANNE. March route from Debussing point to destination, startin at ZERO plus 15.ZERO hour will be the time the last Bus passes debussing point. Intervals of 500 yards between Units will be maintained.

3. The Battalion will parade in Mass on the same ground as yesterday in time to move off at 9.15.a.m.On moving off, Companies will be told off in Bus parties of 25. The signal for "debussing" will be a "G" on bugleon which all ranks will fall in off the right side of the road.

4. Sick men, unable to march, as reported to Battn Headquarters this morning, will parade at Battn Headquarters at 8,45.a.m. under Sgt Morton, who will be provided with a nominal roll and march the party to CROSS ROADS W of the church in BOESEGHEM to arrive there by 9.30.a.m.

5. The whole of the transport will proceed by road, starting at 9.a.m.
ROUTE:- BOESEGHEM - AIRE - MAMETZ - THEROUANNE - to destination.

6. Officers valises will be ready for collection at Battalion and Coy Headquarters by 8.30.a.m. One baggage wagon will collect these, (commencing at "C" Coy H.Q. at 8.30.a.m.) and return to Transport Lines.

7. Blankets in bundles of 10, tied up and labelled, will be at Coy H.Q. by 7.30.a.m. One baggage wagon will collect these (commencing at "C" Coy H.Q. at 7.30.a.m.)and return to Transport Lines.

8. Baggage wagons will march with 1st Line Transport.

9. The Mess Cart will collect Company Mess boxes, commencing with "B" Company, at 8.15.a.m.The Medical Cart will be at Medical Inspection Room (Battn.H.Q.) at 8.30.a.m.

10. Three lorries will be at CROSS ROADS N of third E in BOESEGHEMat 6.30.a.m. tomorrow. Two guides will meet these lorries and conduct two direct to Qr Mr's Stores. The other will call at each Company Headquarters, and Battalion Headquarters, for the extra 100 lbs per Company, and also at the billet of the Band, . . . (No.92.) for the packs and rifles of the Band, which will be ready for loading at 6.30.a.m.
The Band will carry their waterproof sheets. It will also collect stores from Battalion Orderly Room.
The Quartermaster will superintend loading of lorries and proceed with them to destination.

11. Breakfast at 7.a.m. Dinners on arrival (To be cooked en route)

12. ACKNOWLEDGE.

G.H.Williamson. Lieut.A/Adjutant.

2/5th Battalion.The Sherwood Foresters.

Issued at 9.15.p.m.
Distribution.
Copy No.1. C.O.
Copy No.2. 2nd in Command.
Copy No.3. Adjutant.
Copy No.4."A" Coy.
Copy No.5. "B" Coy.
Copy No.6."C" Coy.
Copy.No.7."D" Coy.
Copy.No.8. H.Q.Coy.
Copy No.9. Transport Officer.
Copy No.10. Quartermaster.
Copy No.11. Medical Officer.
Copy No.12. Chaplain.
Copy No.13. R.S.M.
Copy No.14 and 15. File.

OPERATION ORDERS No. 27

by

Major C.R.C. TRENCH, Commanding
2/5th. Battalion, The Sherwood Foresters.

10.10.1917.

Reference Maps HAZEBROUCK, Sheet 5 a
LENS 11.

1. The Battalion will move today by Route March to BAILLEUL and AUCHEL,

2. The Battalion will parade in Mass on the square by the Regtl. Canteen. in time to move off by 11 a.m .
ROUTE. Road Junction by Battalion Orderly Room - ERNY-St.JULIEN FLECHIN - ESTREE - PALFART LEDONCHELLE - DESTINATION.

3. 1st. Line Transport will march immediately in rear of the Battalion. 500 yards intervals will be maintained between the Transport of one Unit and the head of the next Unit. Baggage wagons, when off loaded will rejoin No. 4 Coy., 59th. Divisional Train at BAILLEUL.

4. A rear party consisting of 1 Sergt. and 5 other ranks to be detailed later, will remain behind and travel by the second Motor lorry on the 15th. instant. They will be rationed accordingly They will be responsible for seeing that billets are left clean, and no refuse of any sort is left unburned near the billets.

5. The Billeting party as already detailed under 2nd. Lieut. C. Gandy, will proceed on bicycles or horses to SAINES - LES - PERNES Church, where they will report to the Staff Captain at 12.30 p.m. The Interpreter will also accompany the party. Guides from billeting party will meet their respective Coys. on the outskirts of the billeting area.

6. Officers' Valises and Coy. Mess Boxes will be ready outside
the Officers' Mess of their respective companies by 8.15 a.m.
Blankets in bundles of 10, tied up and labelled will be at
Coy. Hd. Qrs. at 8.15 a.m. Each Company will arrange to
have a guide at Transport Lines by 8 a.m. The wagons and the
Mess Cart will then proceed to Companies in the following order -
"C", "B", "D", "A" and Headquarters.
The guides will travel with the wagon and Mess Cart, until
their respective Coy. is reached. One Officer per Company, will
be detailed to see that these stores are ready at the
specified time.

7. Sick men,, unable to march will parade on road outside Bn. Orderly Room at 9.15 a.m., and will be marched by the Battalion Orderly Sergeant to DELETTE CHURCH, and await an Ambulance. Any men who cannot be carried on an ambulance will return to Battalion Headquarters and will be marched with the slow party.

8. No man will be allowed to fall out without permission in
writing of an Officer. No man will be allowed to enter an
Ambulance without a written order by a Medical Officer.
A party. consisting of Other Ranks, who, in the opinion of the
Officer Commanding Company are unable to march at the same rate
as the Battalion will move, will be formed up prior to moving
off under 2nd. Lieut. W. Binks. The party will march in rear
of the whole column, leaving the square at 11.5 a.m., and any.
men falling out from the Battalion will join this party and not
proceed independently. The names of all men falling out on
the line of march and the reason for so doing will be sent in
to Battalion Orderly Room immediately on arrival at destination.

9. One motor lorry will be provided to carry only necessary stores. On the 15th. instant two more lorries will be provided to remove surplus stores. Lorries will be at COYECQUE Station at 9.0 a.m. to-day and 7 a.m. on the 15th. instant. All surplus stores will be dumped at Quartermaster's Stores by 9.30 a.m., and the rear party will be responsible for guarding same after departure of Battalion.

10. Haversack rations will be carried.

11. The sandbags or packsof the Band will be dumped at the Q.M's. Stores at 8.30 a.m.

12. Acknowledge.

E.E. ANDREWS,
2nd. Lieutenantand A/Adjutant,
2/5th. Battalion, The Sherwood Foresters.

Issued at 7.30 a.m.

DISTRIBUTION.

Copy. No. 1 Commanding Officer.
2 2nd. in Command
3 "A" Coy.
4 "B" Coy.
5. C Coy.
6. "D" Coy.
7 Headquarters Coy.
8 Medical Officer
9 Transport Officer
10 Quartermaster.
11 2nd. Lt. C. Gandy
12 2nd. Lieut. W. Binks
13 Adjutant
14 R.S.M.
15 Interpreter
16. 17 & 18 File.

OPERATION ORDERS No. 22

by

Major C.R.C. TRENCH,

Commanding

2/5th. Battalion. The Sherwood Foresters.

- - - - - - - - - -

1. The Battalion will move by Route March to HERSIN, tomorrow.

2. Companies and Transport will parade as follows at 8.45 am.

"B" Coy. and Transport	At CRUCIFIX
Hd.Qrs. Company	Outside their Headquarters.
"C" Coy. at CROSS ROADS due	WEST of S of Station.
"A" Coy.	Outside their billets.

3. The Medical Officer will notify Companies as to men who are unable to march with the Battalion.

4. The Quartermaster will arrange for Baggage Wagons to report in the following order :-
Transport, "B" Coy., Battalion Headquarters, Headquarters Coy, "C" Coy., "A" Company, commencing at 8 a.m.
The orderly Officer will proceed with wagons to supervise loading. One wagon will be allotted for blankets and one for Officers' Valises.

5. Stores to be carried on lorry will be dumped by 9 a.m. as under :-

Transport and "B" Coy.	Quartermaster's Stores.
Hd.Qrs., "C" & "A" Coys.	Battalion Headquarters.

The quartermaster will arrange for guard to be posted at Battalion Headquarters when Quarter Guard dismounts.

6. The Quartermaster will arrange for guide to be at VALHUON CHURCH at 7 a.m. to meet lorry.

7. A Billeting Party consisting of 2nd. Lieut. W. Hague, Interpreter and one N.C.O. from each Company, will leave Battalion Headquarters at 7.45 a.m. They will take advantage of any lorry proceeding in the same direction.

8. Officers' Mess Cart will collect Mess Boxes, commencing at 8.30 a.m. as follows :-
"B", Hd.Qrs. "C", "A", and will await Transport by "A" Coy.

9. Orderly Officer tomorrow :- 2nd. Lieut. C. WITT.

10 Sick Parade will be held at destination.

F.E. ANDREWS, 2nd. Lieut. & A/Adjt,
2/5th.BATTALION, THE SHERWOOD FORESTERS.

OPERATION ORDER. No. 30.

by

MAJOR. C. R. C. TRENCH.

Commanding 2/5th Battalion. The Sherwood Foresters.

12th Octr. 1917.

1. The Battalion will move by Route March to GOUY - SERVINS tomorrow (about 4 miles)

2. Companies and Transport will parade as follows at 10.30.a.m.
Companies in column of route outside their huts.
Transport:- Head of column on RUE GRANDE.

3. The Medical Officer will notify O.C. 2/3rd North Midland Field Ambulance BARLIN by 9.a.m. as to men who are unable to march with the Battalion. He will also notify Coys concerned that these men are to parade at 62 RUE GRANDE at 9.45.a.m.

4. The Quartermaster will arrange for baggage wagons to report as follows:-
Blanket Wagon. 8.30.a.m. Transport lines.
Then to Quartermaster's Stores, and then to Companies, and to remain with Companies until picked up by Transport.
The Orderly Officer will supervise the loading of this wagon.
Officers valises' wagon - Battalion Headquarters, 8.30.a.m, then to Companies, returning to Quarter Master's Stores. Companies must arrange that blankets are rolled tightly.
Coys will detail guides to report at Transport Lines at 8.15.a.m. to guide wagon to Officers billets.

5. Stores to be carried on lorry will be dumped at Qr Mr's Stores by 9.a.m. The Quartermaster will arrange for a guide to be at BARLIN CHURCH at 7.a.m. to meet lorry.

6. A billeting party consisting of Capt Waterhouse, Interpreter and one N.C.O. from each Company, will leave Qr Mr's Stores at 8.a.m. Packs of billeting party will be carried on lorry.
Capt. Waterhouse will report to Battalion Orderly Room at 7.45.a.m.

7. Officers Mess cart will collect mess boxes commencing at (9.30. a.m.) as follows:- "C" Coy. "B" Coy. "A" Coy. Bn Hd Qrs, and will await Transport at Quarter Master's Stores.

8. Sick parade will be held at destination.

9. The Interpreter will leave the necessary list of Officers, and other ranks billets, at the Battalion Orderly Room by 7.45.a.m.

10. ACKNOWLEDGE.

Sd. F.E. Andrews. 2/Lieut.
A/Adjutant.
2/5th Bn. The Sherwood Foresters.

DISTRIBUTION.

1. Commdg Officer.
2. ~~Capt. F.H.L.~~ Second in Command.
3. Adjutant.
4. "A" Company.
5. "B" Company.
6. "C" Company.
7. "D" Company.
8. Headquarters.
9. Regtl Sgt Major.
10. 2/Lieut. C. Gandy.
11. Capt Waterhouse.
12. Medical Officer.
13. Quarter Master.
14. Transport Officer.
15. Interpreter.
16. File.
17. File.
18. File.

Issued at 9.20.p.m.

SECRET. OPERATION ORDERS NO 31
by
Lieut. Colonel H.R. GADD M.C.,
Commanding
2/5th. Battalion, The Sherwood Foresters.
20.10.1917.

1. The Battalion will relieve the 2/4th. Battalion, Leicester Regiment on the night of the 21 - 22nd. inst.

2. Relief will be carried out as follows :-
"A" Coy. 2/5th. Bn S.F. relieve "A" Coy., 2/4th. Leics.
"B" Coy. 2/5th. Bn. S.F. relieve "B" Coy. 2/4th. Leics.
"C" Coy. 2/5th. Bn. S.F. relieve "D" Coy. 2/4th. Leics.

3. Completion of relief will be reported by the code word "BARNACLE"

4. All Maps , Aeroplane Photos. Trench Stores, Strombos Horns, will be taken over on relief and receipts given, copy of which will be sent to Battalion Headquarters by 10 a.m. 22nd. ins

5. Companies will parade in the CHATEAU Square ready to move off at 4.15 a.m. and will proceed by Decauville Railway to LA COULOTTE.
Guides will be provided at Detraining Point as follows :-
1 Battalion Headquarters.
1 Company Headquarters.
1 per Platoon
1 for R.A.P.

6. Lewis Guns, Ammunition in Magazines, Company Stores, including 6 petrol tins (empty) signalling equipment and Battalion Headquarters Stores will be carried by those responsible on the train.

7. Entraining will take place in the following order :-
Battalion Headquarters
"A" Coy.
"C" Coy.
"B" Coy.
Regimental Aid Post.

8. Officer Commanding "B" Company will detail a N.C.O., who will report to R.S.M. at detraining point. This N.C.O. will remain at Detraining Point in ch arge of any stores that cannot be carried the first journey, and will report to Battalion Headquarters when all stores have been removed. Officers Commanding Companies will indent on O.C. "B" Company for the necessary carrying parties.

9. Companies will arrange for rations for Monday to be issued to Other Ranks before the Battalion entrains. Rations are not to be carried in bulk. A proprtion of Tommy Cookers will be issued.

10. Special maps issued to Company Co manders will be handed in to Battalion Headquarters by 10 a.m. to-morrow.

11. Regimental Aid Post will be at T.a.b.25.75.
(Reference special map).

F.W. SMITH,
Lieutenant and Adjutant,
2/5th. Battalion, The Sherwood Foresters.

SECRET. ORDERS No. 36. Copy No........

by
Lieut.Colonel. H.R.GADD M.C.
Commanding
2/5th Battalion.Sherwood Foresters.

26.10.17.

....

1. Battalion Headquarters will close tomorrow at present situation at 10. a.m. and open at same hour in SUNKEN ROAD at T.2.b.2.9. By day everyone will enter Battalion Headquarters by new Camouflaged Trench from BEAVER West of the SUNKEN ROAD.

2. The present Battalion Headquarters T.3.a.4.1. will be made into a STRONG POINT and will be known as BALBUS and will be garrisoned by the Platoon of "D" Company. The defence of the post will be organised in accordance with instructions issued separately. This Platoon will move into BALBUS tonight.

3. The Headquarters of the Right Front company will move from AVION Trench to T.3.a.4.1. (BALBUS). Two Officers of this Company will live in AVION TRENCH.

G.H.WILLIAMSON,
Lieut and Adjutant.

Distribution.
Normal
Plus
178th Inf Bde.
2/7th Sher Fors.

APPENDIX.
to
OPERATION ORDERS No 32

28.10.17.

Companies will take over accommodation as follows:-

No1 Dugout C Coy.H.Q. 2/5th from C Coy H.Q. 2/7th

2. " Three Platoons C Coy 2/5th from C Coy H.Q. 2/7th

3 " Batt H.Q. 2/5th from Batt H.Q. 2/7th
A Coy H.Q. " " B & D Coy H.Q. 2/7th.
1 Platoon A Coy 2/5th from 1 Platoon D Coy 2/7th.
2 Platoons A Coy " " 2 Platoons B Coy "

5 " Two Platoons B Coy 2/5th from 2 Platoons A Coy 2/7th
One Platoon B Coy " " 1 " D " "

6 " B Coy H.Q. 2/5th From A Coy H.Q. 2/7th

Reinforcements of 2/5th and 2/7th will remain in No 3 dugout and No 5 dugout.

Distribution.
2 copies per coy.

G.W. WILLIAMSON.
Lieut and Adjutant.

OPERATION ORDERS No. [illegible].
by
Lieut.Colonel.H.R.GADD M.C.
Commanding.
2/5th Battalion.Sherwood Foresters.

** 29.10.17.

Reference Map 36c S.W. 1/20.000.

1. The Battalion will be relieved by the 2/7th Battalion on night of 29/30th October, and on relief will proceed to quarters reconnoitred today in Support Line.

2. By 7 p.m. 29th inst., The Front Line will be taken over by "A" & "C" Coys as on night of 26/27th ("D" Coy returning to position of Coy in Support).

3. Relief will take place as follows:-

<u>In The Line</u> As arranged by O.C. 2/7th Battn.

<u>In Support.</u> Companies will proceed by platoons to position in support line as shown on Appendix.

4. Guides will be provided as follows:-

For Battn.H.Q.2/7th..		1.	
" "A" Coy	"	2	(1 for Coy H.Q. & 1 for Platoon)
" "B" "	"	4	(1 " " " " 3 " Platoons)
"C" "	"	2	(1 " " ")
"D" "	"	4	(1 " " " & 3 " ")
R.A.P.	"	1.	

Guides will be at junction of BEAVER and CYRIL at 6.30 p.m. O.C. "A" Coy will detail one Officer to be at that point in charge of the guides.
O's C Coys will be responsible for giving each guide written instructions as to his duties.

5. O's.C. Coys will detail one Officer per Company and one man per Platoon to proceed before noon to the Support Line. These details will act as guides and will be at junction of CYRIL and RED TRENCH by 6.30 p.m. Officers will be provided with a copy of APPENDIX and will be responsible that the Companies are taken direct to their quarters.

6. Completion of relief will be reported to Batt.H.Q. by Code Words ("Your O.S. 10.received").

7. All maps, trench stores, petrol tins etc., will be handed over and receipts taken. Copies will be forwarded to Batt H.Q. by 10. a.m. 30th inst.

8. Officers as detailed ~~xxxx~~ in para 5 will arrange for tea and rum to be ready for issue to men on arrival at new quarters.
The Quartermaster has instructions to send up all tea in bulk to Companies, which will thus be available for drawing before other rations.
These officers will also arrange for a guide to be available to take ration party to dump, after packs have been left in new quarters. Rations will be drawn immediately after arrival.

9. Companies will arrange for all stores that are to be taken to new area, be carried down during the day. These carrying parties will await arrival of Companies in new area.
No more than SIX Other Ranks will be detailed per Company and they will proceed in parties of not more than three.

4yt [illegible]
War Diary.

P. T. O.

10. In the new Area Companies will act as follows on instructions from Battn. H.Q. in case of enemy attack:-

Battalion Headquarters will proceed to LA COULOTTE

one Platoon (D Coy) will proceed up CYRIL and BEAVER Trenches and report to O.C. 2/7th Battalion.

"A" Coy will take over the following Posts in ADEPT TRENCH A.B.C. & D.E.F.
"B" Coy will take over G.H.J.K.L.M.

Officers Commanding Companies will arrange to reconnoitre these posts by 6 p.m. 30th inst. Further instructions for action in case of attack will be issued later.

11. Acknowledge.

Issued at 12. 45 am.

Distribution.

G.H. WILLIAMSON.
Lieut and Adjutant.

Normal Plus
2/7th Battalion.
176th Inf Bde.

11

Army Form C. 2118.

WAR DIARY
or
INTELLIGENCE SUMMARY
(Erase heading not required.)

Instructions regarding War Diaries and Intelligence Summaries are contained in F. S. Regs., Part II. and the Staff Manual respectively. Title Pages will be prepared in manuscript.

2/5 Notts & Derby

Nov 17 Vol 10

Place	Date	Hour	Summary of Events and Information	Remarks and references to Appendices
[illegible]	1917 Nov 1.		Battalion in Red Trench Support by Lens.	[initials]
	2		Batt in Red Trench.	[initials]
	3.		Reconnoitring by officers in contemplated raid on Bosch lines. Batt still in Red Trench.	[initials]
	4.		Raiding Party withdrawn to SOUCHEZ. Batt in Red Trench	[initials]
	5		Practices at Souchez carried out by Raiding Party.	[initials]
	6.		Batt relieved by 2/6. South Staffs and proceeded to SOUCHEZ Camp	[initials]
	7		Time spent in cleaning up and kit inspection.	[initials]
	[illegible]		Raid on METAL TRENCH between N 33 d. 2. 70 and N 33 d 45. 53 unsuccessful. Bangalore Torpedo left in No Mans Land.	[initials]
	[illegible]		Improvements to treatments carried out under [illegible] arrangements. Working parties supplied under Bde orders.	[initials]

2449 Wt. W14957/M90 750,000 1/16 J.B.C. & A. Forms/C.2118/12.

Instructions regarding War Diaries and Intelligence Summaries are contained in F. S. Regs., Part II. and the Staff Manual respectively. Title Pages will be prepared in manuscript.

WAR DIARY
or
INTELLIGENCE SUMMARY
(Erase heading not required.)

Army Form C. 2118.

Place	Date	Hour	Summary of Events and Information	Remarks and references to Appendices
Souchez, Nov 6	1917. Nov 10		Battalion bathed at Carency. NCOs class commenced.	JM
	11.		Divine Services. Divisional Staff Ride under G.O.C. Division. Tactical Scheme for officers under Major French at 1.30pm.	JM
	12.		Coy training. Presentation of decorations to officers & men by G.O.C. Division for operations 26.9.17.	JM
	13.		Tactical Scheme for C & D Coys under C.O. A Coy bathing & on duty for fatigue. B Coy bathing. Kit inspection afternoon.	JM
	14.		Battalion moved to Verdun Camp, Agnez-les-Duisans.	JM
	15.		Coys at disposal of O.C. Coys for morning. Afternoon - Tactical Scheme for all officers under C.O.	JM
	16.		Coy training. 1 Coy on Range near ETRUN.	JM
	17.		Tactical Exercise for all Coys except D allotted range. Afternoon - Bathing.	JM

2449 Wt. W14957/M90 750,000 1/16 J.B.C. & A. Forms/C.2118/12.

Instructions regarding War Diaries and Intelligence Summaries are contained in F. S. Regs., Part II. and the Staff Manual respectively. Title Pages will be prepared in manuscript.

WAR DIARY
or
INTELLIGENCE SUMMARY

(Erase heading not required.)

Army Form C. 2118.

Place	Date	Hour	Summary of Events and Information	Remarks and references to Appendices
	1917 Nov 18		Divine Services. Inspection of all Rifles and Bayonets by C.O. Lewis Gun practice on Range.	JA
	19		Coys at disposal of Coy Commanders. Tactical Scheme for all officers and N.C.O.s except C.S.M.s at 9.30 am. Batt. left for Blairville at 4 pm and arrived 9.25 pm.	JA
	20		3/4 hr P.T. and remainder of morning preparing for move at 1 hours notice.	JA
	21		Batt. left Blairville for Gomiecourt at 8.30 pm and arrived 12.45 am	JA
	22		C.O and Coy Commanders reconnoitred freshly captured ground by Ribecourt. Batt. resting. Weather very wet.	JA
	23		Batt. left Gomiecourt at 11 am for Equancourt. Marched to Bihucourt West and entrained at 12 noon. Detrained Ytres and marched to Equancourt.	JA

Army Form C. 2118.

Instructions regarding War Diaries and Intelligence Summaries are contained in F. S. Regs., Part II. and the Staff Manual respectively. Title Pages will be prepared in manuscript.

WAR DIARY
or
INTELLIGENCE SUMMARY

(Erase heading not required.)

Place	Date	Hour	Summary of Events and Information	Remarks and references to Appendices
Equancourt	Nov 24		Battalion bathed. Coy training carried out.	[illegible]
	25		Divine Services. Inspection of billets by C.O. Musketry and rifle inspection during morning.	[illegible]
	26		Batn left Equancourt for Marcoing. Left at 9.15 am and arrived at 3 pm.	[illegible]
Marcoing	27		A Coy working party under W. Riding Field Coy R.E. Batn left for Equancourt at 2 hours notice. Left by Platoons at ¼ hr intervals.	[illegible]
Equancourt	28		Batn bathed and preparations made for active measures.	[illegible]
Trescault	29		Btn moved from Equancourt to support line by Trescault.	[illegible]
	30.		Bt. moved up from trenches by Trescault from L 20 d 5 3 to L 32 b central approx.	[illegible]

[illegible signature] Lt. Col.
Comdg. 1/5 Notts & Derby Regt.

2449 Wt. W14957/M90 750,000 1/16 J.B.C. & A. Forms/C.2118/12.

Confidential

Instructions regarding War Diaries and Intelligence Summaries are contained in F. S. Regs., Part II. and the Staff Manual respectively. Title Pages will be prepared in manuscript.

WAR DIARY
or
INTELLIGENCE SUMMARY
(Erase heading not required.)

Army Form C. 2118.

2/5 Sherwood Foresters

Vol 11

Place	Date 1917	Hour	Summary of Events and Information	Remarks and references to Appendices
TRESCAULT	Dec 1.		Batn moved back to SUPPORT LINE by TRESCAULT. Relieved by K.S.L.I. During early part of evening one Coy. ordered to cover RIBECOURT – MARCOING Road owing to inform. recd that MARCOING had been evacuated.	JA
	2.		Batn in old HINDENBURG FRONT LINE and resting for one day. Slight gas shelling during afternoon behind left flank of Batn.	JA
	3.		Batn. in Hindenburg Front line. Orders issued for relief of 2/5 North Staffs cancelled.	JA OO No 41
	4.		Btn. moved from HINDENBURG FRONT LINE to OLD English Front Line by BILHEM FARM. Several aerial bombs dropped on Batn area. 1 man injured.	JA OO 42
	5.		Btn. moved suddenly to fill up gap in line S.E. of FLESQUIRES. Batn. Hd. Qrs. in German Dug-out set on fire by petrol. All papers destroyed in Orderly Room. Batn working all night consolidating front.	JA
	6.		Batn. resting during morning & afternoon. Attack by Bosch on our left flank repelled very easily. Btn. working all night digging posts (front line).	JA
	7		Slight barrage about 5.30 am. by Bosch. Two destructive shoots carried out by our Artillery between 3 & 4 pm & 6 & 7 am. Btn. working all night consolidating & wiring.	JA

2449 Wt. W14957/M90 750,000 1/16 J.B.C. & A. Forms/C.2118/12.

Army Form C. 2118.

Instructions regarding War Diaries and Intelligence Summaries are contained in F. S. Regs., Part II. and the Staff Manual respectively. Title Pages will be prepared in manuscript.

WAR DIARY
or
INTELLIGENCE SUMMARY

(Erase heading not required.)

Place	Date 1917	Hour	Summary of Events and Information	Remarks and references to Appendices
FLESQUIRES	Dec 8.		Battn resting during day. Inspections of rifles by Coys. Battn working under Coy arrangements during night improving comfort of line. Concentration shoot as on previous day at same times.	[initials]
	9.		Battn less "C" Coy and 8 L. Gun teams relieved by 14th D.L.I. & proceeded to CATACOMB at RIBECOURT. All Battn working digging C.T.s.	[initials] 0047
RIBECOURT.	10.		Battn. less C Coy & L.G. teams in CATACOMB all day. C Coy & teams rejoined at 9.30 pm. "D" Coy proceeded to trenches at K35b at 9 pm. The day spent in rifle cleaning & foot rubbing etc.	[initials] 0047
	11.		Battn less "D" Coy left RIBECOURT by platoons commencing at 3.15 am for trenches at K35b. Remainder of day improving accommodation & building trench shelters.	[initials] 0048
	12.		Working Party of 200 at K24. Remainder of Battn improving trenches.	[initials]
	13.		Battn on Working Party and improving accommodation.	[initials]
	14.		Battn. moving Bosch wire from rear to front of trenches & improving own trenches	[initials]
	15.		B & C Coys went LECHELLE for Bathing. A & D Coy on W.P. on Communication Trenches.	[initials] 0049

2449 Wt. W14957/M90 750,000 1/16 J.B.C. & A. Forms/C.2118/12.

Army Form C. 2118.

Instructions regarding War Diaries and Intelligence Summaries are contained in F. S. Regs., Part II. and the Staff Manual respectively. Title Pages will be prepared in manuscript.

WAR DIARY
or
INTELLIGENCE SUMMARY
(Erase heading not required.)

Place	Date	~~Hour~~	Summary of Events and Information	Remarks and references to Appendices
	Dec.	16.	Interchange of Position of Coys. A & D Coys ~~proceeded to Bertincourt~~ B & C returned from Lechelle. Court of Enquiry at 7th Bde Hd Qrs re fire on 5/6th night.	[initials] O.O. No 50
		17	2 Coys. A & D at BERTINCOURT for bathing. ~~B & C returned to Nurlu... Lane K35...~~ W.P. 4 Offs & 100 ORs supplied for W.P. for 3 hours.	[initials]
		18.	A & D Coys returned from Bertincourt. W.P. of 4 NCOs & 70 men supplied at Bgde Hd Qrs Q4 d 8.3. Battn moved to trenches K34 a & b K35 a relieving 2/8 S.F.	[initials] O.O. No 51
		19.	Clearing trenches of rubbish & erecting trench shelters. 8 Platoons on W.P. digging CT & wiring front line N. East of FLESQUIRES 2 Casualties.	[initials]
		20.	Bn moved to BARASTRE relieved by 7th Border Regt. Relief complete by 7.30 pm	[initials] O.O. No 52
BARASTRE		21	Bn cleaning up and resting. Clothing Board held.	[initials]
		22.	P.T. for 3/4 hour in morning. Inspections of kit and cleaning up	[initials]
		23.	Btn. moved to BEAULENCOURT. Left 10.30 am Arrived 11.50 am. Afternoon – Resting	[initials] O.O. No 53
BEAULENCOURT.		24.	1 hour Saluting drill – Divine Service 9.45 am. Commn. services (voluntary) during day. Transport moved to BAPAUME by road	[initials] O.O. No 54
		25	Battn entrained BAPAUME 8.30 am for PETIT HOUVIN. Marched to HOUVIN HOUVIGNEUL. Arrived 1.50 pm.	[initials]

2449 Wt. W14957/M90 750,000 1/16 J.B.C. & A. Forms/C.2118/12.

Army Form C. 2118.

Instructions regarding War Diaries and Intelligence Summaries are contained in F. S. Regs., Part II. and the Staff Manual respectively. Title Pages will be prepared in manuscript.

WAR DIARY
or
INTELLIGENCE SUMMARY

(Erase heading not required.)

Place	Date	Hour	Summary of Events and Information	Remarks and references to Appendices
HOUVIN-HOUVIGNEUL	Dec 26		Battn. clearing up snow from Billets and roads.	[initials]
	27		Preps. for Xmas dinner. Dinner at 2 pm Concert 4 pm. Officers dinner 8 pm. Road clearing during morning	[initials]
	28		Battn training. Marching + Saluting. P.T. training.	[initials]
	29		B Coy sent to DOULLENS at 3 am for clearing snow on Railway Remainder of Battn. on road-clearing between Houvin-Houvigneul and Etree-Wamin.	[initials]
	30.		Divine Service 9.45 am. Cards of Commendation presented to Brigade at 10.45 am	[initials]
	31.		Battn training P.T. + B.F. Musketry. - Saluting. 1 Coy Bgde Fatigue clearing B.F. Course.	[initials]

H R Gadd Lt Col
Comdg. 2/5th BATTn. NOTTS & DERBY REGT.

2449 Wt. W14957/M90 750,000 1/16 J.B.C. & A. Forms/C.2118/12.

Copy No..........

OPERATION ORDERS No41.
by
Lieut. Colonel. H.R.GADD. M.C.
Commanding
2/5th Battalion. Sherwood Foresters.

3.12.17.

1. The Battalion will relieve the 2/5th North Staffs in FLESQUIRES to-day.

2. Relief will take place as under:-

2/5th Sherwoods.	2/5th North Staffs.
"A" Coy.	"C" Coy.
"B" "	"B" "
"C" "	"A" "
"D" "	"D" "

3. Guides will be sent to Companies before moving off.

4. Companiesx will move across country in Artillery formation, no larger column thant Half a Platoon, Companies leaving their present position as under;-
"A" Coy. 3 p.m. H.Q. Coy. 3.5 p.m. "B" Coy. 3.15 p.m.
"B" " 3.20 p.m. "C" " 3.30 p.m.

5. Kitchens and water carts will proceed to FLESQUIRES under axxaxxs orders of Transport Officer. They will be located about K.34 a 76
The Horses will be at prsent position of Battalion at 3 p.m.
1 G.S. Wagon per Company and one for Headquarters for L.Guns, Stores, kits etc., will be at present Trenches at 3 p.m.
All surplus Kits, Mess Boxes. Tools etc., will be removd to Q.M. Stores at same time.

6. On arrival in new Trenches, Guides will be provided by Companies to take the Relieved Battalion back to this Battalion's present Trenches.

7. Battalion Headquarters will beK.24.a.1.5.
Brigade Headquarters will be K.29.d.1.5.
Water Cart filling will be in FLESQUIRES near the A.D.S.

8. The role of B & C Coys will be to hold the line in front of the village and the Village defences at all costs.
A & D Coys will be in rserve, and will be at the disposal of G.O.C. of the Brigade in the Line.

9. ACKNOWLEDGE.

(sgd) F%E%ANDREWS.
2nd Lieut & Adjutant.

ISSUED AT........
DISTRIBUTION.

No.1. "A" Coy. No.2. "B" Coy. No.3. "C" Coy.
4. "D" Coy. 5. H.Q. Coy. 6. C.O.
7. R%S%M% 8. M.O. 9. T.O.
10. File and Adjutant. No.12 & 13 War Diary.
14. O.C. 2/5th North Staffs.

Copy. No....

OPERATION ORDERS No 42.
by
Lieut. Colonel. H.R.GADD. M.C.
Commanding
2/5th Battalion. Sherwood Foresters.
.... 4.12.17.

Reference Map. MOEUVRES (Special).

1. The Battalion will move tonight to the Old British Lines North of TRESCAULT.

2. Companies on arrival will be accommodated as under:)

"A" & H.Q. Companies	In the Trench immediately to the East of the "TIP CEMETRY" Road.
"B" Company	In Sap B and OLDHAM ALLEY.
"C" "	BLACKBURN ALLEY. C SAP. BURNLEY AVENUE and D.SAP.
"D" "	In TRESCAULT Trench to the West of the above Road.
Batt.H.Qrs & R.A.P.	Will be in TRESCAULT Trench immediately East of Cemetry.
Kitchens and Water Carts	will be located immediately West of Cemetry.

3. Companies will move off in the following order:-
H.Q. "D" "C" "B" "A".
Route being:- Track K.35 a.- T in TIP.
Times of moving off will benotified later.
Guides are already with the Companies.
Hairy Coats will be worn.
Lewis Guns and 16 Magazines per Gun will be carried.

4. Stores, Trench Kits. will be loaded on the Company Lewis Gun Wagons on receipt of orders. The wagons with Field Kitchens and water carts will proceed under the orders of the Transport ~~Officer ROUTE~~ Officer. RouteK.36 c.0.2.- TRESCAULT-REGENT CRATER.
Times for moving off will be notified later.

5. ACKNOWLEDGE.

(sgd) F.E.ANDREWS.
2nd Lieut. & A/Adjutant.

issued at............

DISTRIBUTION.

Copy No1. Commanding Officer.
2. "A" Company.
3. "B" "
4. "C" Coy.
5. "D" "
6. H.Qrs.
7. File and Adjutant.
8. Medical Officer.
9. Transport Officer.
10. R.S.M.
11 & 12 War Diary.

Copy No 8.

[illegible] 57c   to Col A.R. [illegible] MC   [illegible]

1. The Battalion less C Coy and [illegible] of A and D Coys will be relieved tonight by the 14 DLI and will go into Reserve at the CATACOMBES at RIBECOURT.

2. D Coy will be relieved by a Coy of the 11th ESSEX. All arrangements being made between OC D Coy and OC 11th ESSEX.

3. At 4.30pm tonight C Coy will occupy OUTPOST LINE from the BEET-ROOT FACTORY to [illegible] and will consolidate there. They will come under orders of 14 DLI and will continue there until DLI are relieved. Coy HQ [illegible] will be in OLD FRONT LINE. C Coy will report to [illegible] [illegible] [illegible] WOOD [illegible] NEAR

4. Guides [illegible] (1 per Platoon [illegible]) will be at junction of trench and road [illegible] at 6.30pm and will conduct the DLI to the present position of these Coys. [illegible] "Much BETTER"

5. A & D Coys will leave their [illegible] and ammunition under the command of the DLI and [illegible] Tools (other than [illegible]) and Trench Stores are to be handed over to the DLI and receipts obtained.

6/ On completion of [illegible] the Platts [illegible] responsible for digging C.T. continuation of STATION AVENUE [illegible] [illegible] SUTPAT [illegible]. Trench will be made at least 5' deep and 3' wide at bottom and the sides [illegible] [illegible] off. The three Coys will work under supervision of Capt STABBING and no Coy will leave until the work is completed. Additional tools may be drawn from Bn Hd Qrs but the same number as drawn from Bn Hd Qrs are to be returned to the CATACOMBES.

7/ Rations tonight will be delivered at the CATACOMBES and [illegible] [illegible] ready for [illegible] to Coys immediately on their arrival. C Coy rations will be dumped at C Coys present Hd Qrs. C Coy drawing the Typhoons [illegible] [illegible] [illegible] [illegible] up tomorrow under Coy arrangements.

8/ All Kits Mess Stores etc. will be carried down under Coy arrangements.

9/ Acknowledge

Distribution

A
1 B
2 C
3 D
4 Hd Qrs
5 [illegible]
8 2nd in C

Adjt
9 1st Inf Brigade
10 14 [illegible]

E Andrews
2nd Lt a/Adjt.

SECRET. No 10

Operation Orders No 4

Lt Col [illegible] MC

Map A.[illegible]

1. The Battn will move to UNSEEN TRENCH K 35 early tomorrow morning.

2. Coys will leave the CATACOMBS as follows and spaced by Platoons.

[illegible] 3 [illegible]
B 3 45 [illegible]
A 4 [illegible]
C 4 15 [illegible]

Route will be notified later
Coys will carry with them [illegible] [illegible] and [illegible] proportion of Ammunition.
Platoons will move [illegible] end of [illegible] and [illegible] [illegible] [illegible] [illegible] outside the CATACOMBS.

3. On arrival in UNSEEN TRENCH Coys will stand to in positions allotted to them. During "stand to" accommodation will be allotted to them.

4. Rations and 1 Blanket per man will be [illegible] at [illegible] 35 c 2 6. and will be distributed [illegible]

5. Stand to [illegible] Wagons as under will [illegible] at [illegible] at 3 30 am, at which time all [illegible] will be there ready for [illegible].
The [illegible] will [illegible] the [illegible] [illegible]

Wagons are allotted as under:-

1 per Coy for Lewis Gun Stores Officers and other [illegible]

1 for Hd Qrs Kits and Signals

1 for Tools Medical Stores

1 for Petrol Tins.

5 Coys. will leave their present billets clean and all urine and other tins will be emptied.

6 Acknowledge.

Issued at 10.30 pm

E. Andrews
2nd Lt. & A/Adjt.

Distribution.

1 A
2 B
3 C
4 D
5 H.Q. Coy.
6 C.O.
7 2nd i/c
8 Q.M.
9 File
10 War Diary.

[illegible] 8

Operation Order No [illegible]

by

Lt Col [illegible] M C

Commanding

2/5th Battalion The Sherwood Foresters.

[illegible] 1917

Reference map 57c.

[illegible]

1. "B" & "C" Coys [illegible] LECHELLE [illegible] disposed as under

"B" Coy to [illegible] accommodation in Camp occupied by 2/4th [illegible]

"C" Coy to [illegible] accommodation in Camp occupied by 2/4 [illegible]

2. The route will be TRESCAULT - METZ-en-Couture - NEUVILLE - ~~[illegible]~~ Cross roads [illegible] - LECHELLE.

3. Companies will move off as under in parties not more than 10 at a time, [illegible] platoons by Transport Lines (Q [illegible]). From here they will march by platoons to N W end of METZ, where Coys will reform and march with 200 yards interval between Coys to Destination.

"C" Coy 7 am

"B" Coy and HQs 7 15 am

4. All Coy Stores, Lewis Guns, Lewis Gun ammunition, Officers' Kits, etc. will be dumped at new Ration Dump by 6 am, and will be loaded as soon as limbers arrive. Limbers will then proceed to N W end of METZ where they will [illegible] their respective companies and proceed with them to new area. [illegible] will ~~[illegible]~~ supervise loading, and ensure departure of limbers by 6 30 am.

5. 2nd Lt [illegible] and 1 N C O and 2 [illegible] per Coy will leave for new area at 5 30 am. He will arrange accommodation for Coys with respective Units, and will send guide to meet Coys at [illegible] C.11. Rendezvous for Coy representatives [illegible] R [illegible]

6. Two Company Cookers and 1 Water Cart will [illegible] to new area. Rations for [illegible] will be delivered there. Companies will make own arrangements for carrying of rations today by the men.

P T O

7. When "B" & "C" Coys move "A" Coy will immediately take over accommodation at present occupied by "D" in addition to its present accommodation, and "D" Coy will move back and take over accommodation evacuated by "B" & "C" Coys.
"A" & "D" Coys will each arrange to have at least 3 men told off to guard the dug-outs of Companies into which they are moving.
Companies will at once report alteration of their Report Centres

8. Acknowledge.

J K Andrews
Lieut & Adjutant

Issued at am

Distribution

Copy No. 1 "A" Coy
2 "B" Coy
3 "C" Coy
4 "D" Coy
5 HQ Coy
6 Lieut. Channing
7 Commanding Officer
8 File

12

Operation Orders No. [illegible]
by
Lt-Colonel A. [illegible]
Commanding
2/5th [illegible] 15/12/17.

Reference Maps [illegible]

1. "A" & "D" Coys and [illegible] from H.Q. Coy will [illegible] BERTINCOURT [illegible] of Capt. T. [illegible] Stebbing [illegible] [illegible]
"A" [illegible] and H.Q. [illegible] accommodation in Camp [illegible] 2/4th [illegible]
"D" [illegible] accommodation [illegible] [illegible] billets.
[illegible] "C" Coys will return to [illegible] at 7.30 a.m. All [illegible] [illegible] will proceed to BERTINCOURT & take over command of "A" & "D" Coys on arrival.

2. The route will [illegible] RUYAULCOURT - Destination.

3. Coys will move at [illegible] [illegible] [illegible] parties [illegible] [illegible] reform into Platoons [illegible] [illegible]
From here they will march by Platoons to N.W. end of METZ where Coys will [illegible] [illegible] half Battalion to Destination.
"D" Coy 9.0 a.m.
"A" and H.Q.s 9.15 a.m.
The [illegible] [illegible] transport [illegible] [illegible] its position in front of leading Platoon of "D" Coy [illegible] [illegible] from [illegible]

4. Limber and a half are available for each Company. [illegible] Lewis Guns L.G. Ammunition Officers' Kits etc. will be dumped at [illegible] Dump at 8 a.m. [illegible] loaded as soon as [illegible] arrive. Limbers will report at dump [illegible] commencing at 8 a.m. and as soon as loaded will [illegible] wait with intervals between each from one another. They will then proceed to [illegible] and await arrival of their respective Coys, and will move with them to [illegible]
C.S.M. Brown will supervise loading [illegible] departure of limbers.

5. Both "A" & "D" Coys [illegible] detail 1 NCO + 2 men to report to [illegible] [illegible] [illegible] at 7 a.m.
[illegible] will precede the Battalion and arrange accommodation for the [illegible] [illegible] each Coy will be sent [illegible] [illegible] the [illegible]

6. Coy Cookers and Cooks will accompany [illegible] [illegible]. The Cookers will join Coys as they pass the Transport [illegible] proceed independently and will [illegible]
"D" Coy will be responsible for sending a guide to meet [illegible] [illegible] new area.

7. Rations for tomorrow [illegible] Coys will make their own arrangements for this with Transport allotted to them.

8. 'C' Coy will return to D Coy's present quarters. 'B' Coy will return to [illegible] Hd Qrs to their respective Sections.
A & D Coys will each [illegible] to guard the Dug-outs pending the arrival of [illegible]. These men will also act as guides to incoming companies.
They will not proceed to BERTINCOURT till [illegible] Coy. which occupies the billets they are guarding. Rations for these men will be [illegible].

9. The detachment at BERTINCOURT will be [illegible] for communication with the Batt. [illegible] will always be.

10. All Petrol tins and Stoppers will be collected and dumped by Batt. [illegible] by 5.30 am tomorrow.

11. ACKNOWLEDGE.

Issued at pm.

Distribution

(1) A Coy
(2) B Coy
(3) Hd Qrs Coy
(4) 2nd in C.
(5) T.O. & Qr master.
(6) C.S.M. [illegible]
(7) C. Coy
(8) D Coy
(9) [illegible]
(10) [illegible]

J. Andrews

2nd Lt & Adjt.

[illegible] ORDER No.1.
by
Lieut. Colonel. [illegible]. [illegible].
Commanding
2/5th Battalion Sherwood Foresters.

.... 17.12.17.

WARNING ORDER No.1.

1. The Battalion will relieve the 2/8th Battalion Sherwood Foresters in the Hindenburg ~~Line~~ Front and Support Line in K.[illegible] a & b. and K 35 a on the night of the 18/19th inst at a time to be notified later.

2. "A" Company will take over accommodation occupied by 2/8th Batt'n Sherwood Foresters between Sunken Road K.35 a and present position of our "C" Company.
"C" Company will remain in present position with exception of Dugout immediately EAST of the present R.A.P. but plus remainder of accommodation in new R.A.P. K.35 a.l.1
"B" & "D" Coys will take over accommodation occupied by the remaining three Companies of 2/8th Sherwood Foresters.

3. O.C. "B" Company will be responsible for reconnoitring and allotting accommodation allotted to "B" & "D" Coys.
O.C. "C" Coys will be responsible for reconnoitring and allotting accommodation allotted to "A" Company.

4. All Trench Shelters will be taken from the present line to new lines.
Should Coys have more trench shelters than they require they will return surplus to Battalion Headquarters.

5. Battalion Headquarters will be at present R.A.P. K.35 a.10.25.

6. ACKNOWLEDGE.

Sgd. F.E.ANDREWS.
2nd Lieut & Adjutant.

War D.

OPERATION ORDERS No 51.
by
Lieut. Colonel. H. R. GADD M.C.
Commanding
2/5th Battalion. Sherwood Foresters.

18.12.17.

1. The Battalion will relieve the 2/8th Battalion The Sherwood Foresters in UNSEEN and UNSEEN Support Trenchesin K.34 a & b and K 35 a.
Companies will move off independently in time to be in new area by 4 p.m.

2. All Trench Shelters will be taken from present trenches and re-erected in new trenches.
Any surplus shelters will be returned to new Battalion Hdqrs.

3. Battalion Headquarters will close at 3 p.m. and re-open at dugout immediately East of present R.A.P., K.35 a. 10.25 at same time.

4. Companies will report giving location of their Report Centres to New Battalion Headquarters as soon as relief is complete.

5. **ACKNOWLEDGE**

(sgd) F.E. ANDREWS.
2nd Lieut & Adjutant.
2/5th Battalion. The Sherwood Foresters.

Issued at 3 p.m.

Distribution.

Copy. No 1. "A" Coy.
2. "B" "
3. "C" "
4. "D" "
5. H.Q.
6. R.S.M.
7. M.O.
8. File.

Operation Orders No. [illegible]
by
Lt-Colonel [illegible]
Commanding
2/5th Bn. the [illegible]

20-12-17

Ref. MAPS 57c

1. The Battalion will be relieved tomorrow by the [illegible] and [illegible] Camps at BARASTRE.

2. [illegible] 1 for Bn [illegible] and one per Coy, and 1 for R.A.P. [illegible] detailed [illegible] and H.Q. [illegible] will report at Bn. H.Q. at [illegible] per Platoon (16) [illegible] Harness [illegible] Bn. H.Q. at 12 noon. [illegible] will carry harnessed [illegible]. DRESS: Great Coats [illegible] packs.

3. Lt. Y.W. Smith and 2 men per [illegible] and [illegible] from Transport will [illegible] Bn. H.Q. at 8.5 am and proceed to BARASTRE as Billeting Party. They will meet Capt. [illegible] there at [illegible] H.Q. at 8 am. They will pick up the Transport man as they pass.

[illegible] The relief Coys will [illegible] at least 200 [illegible] interval being maintained between Coys. ROUTE: [illegible] Any as [illegible] as RUYAULCOURT, then [illegible] BARASTRE. Coys will march by Sections [illegible] WEST of HAVRINCOURT WOOD.

Blankets, kits and surplus stores will be [illegible] by 10 am. by which time Transport Officer will [illegible] sufficient waggons to remove it. The R.S.M. will superintend [illegible] (C[illegible] at Bn. Ration Dump).

(b) All [illegible] Mess kits will be at Bn. Ration Dump [illegible] at which time the Mess Cart will be loaded. [illegible] will superintend the loading.

(c) Coy. L.G. [illegible] will be at Coy. Ration Dumps at 3 pm and will accompany respective Coys.

(d) Officers will inform Bn. H.Q. by 9.30 am when and where they [illegible] charge.

[illegible] Trenches and [illegible] will be left [illegible] and all stores will be handed over and [illegible]

[illegible] On the march [illegible] to march [illegible] and [illegible] will [illegible] be carried.

Hairy Coats may be worn or not at the discretion of Coy. Commanders.

8. When relieved and before moving off, Companies will send the Code Word "BACCHUS" to Bn H.Q.

9. Transport lines will [illegible] under orders of Transport Officer.

10. Acknowledge.

Issued at 12.30 a.m.

[illegible]
Capt & Adjutant

Distribution

Copy No.	
1	C.O.
2	Adjt
3	'A' Coy
4	'B' "
5	'C' "
6	'D' "
7	H.Q. "
8	M.O.
9	Transport Officer & Q.M.
10	Lt. W.W. Smith
11	R.S.M.
12	177th Infy Bde
13	178th " "
14	File
15 & 16	War Diary

OPERATION [illegible] ORDER [illegible] No. [illegible]

by

Lieutenant-Colonel [illegible] [illegible] D.S.O.,

Commanding

[illegible] Battalion, The Sherwood Foresters.

[illegible] [illegible] 1 [illegible]

1. [illegible] The Battalion will march [illegible] to [illegible] [illegible].

2. [illegible] The Battalion will [illegible] on [illegible] [illegible] road and move off at 10.10 a.m.
DRESS - Marching Order. [illegible] [illegible]
[illegible] pack [illegible] [illegible]
ROUTE - [illegible]-AU-BOIS.

3. [illegible] The following [illegible] [illegible] will [illegible] [illegible] the Battalion :-
Field Kitchens
Water Carts
Mess Carts
Medical Cart
[illegible] [illegible] [illegible] [illegible].

4. STORES. The Quartermaster will arrange with the [illegible] Officer for the [illegible] of [illegible].

5. KITS. Kits will be stacked at Quartermaster's Stores as follows:
(a) Blankets by [illegible] a.m.
(b) Officers' Kits [illegible] a.m.
(c) Mess Kits [illegible] a.m.
The R.Q.M.S. will superintend the stacking of these, and the Quartermaster will arrange with the Transport Officer for their transport.

6. SLOW PARTY. The slow party will march under the [illegible] Officer, and will parade at the Battalion [illegible] at 10 a.m.

7. INSPECTION. The Commanding Officer will inspect all [illegible] and Lines at [illegible] a.m.

8. DISCIPLINE. The strictest march discipline will be observed. The attention of all concerned is called to the orders as to [illegible] [illegible] [illegible] on the line of march.

9. ACKNOWLEDGE.

[illegible] [illegible]
[illegible] Adjutant,
[illegible] Battalion, The Sherwood Foresters.

ISSUED AT

DISTRIBUTION

Copy No. 1 Commanding Officer.
2 "A" Company.
3 "B" Company.
4 "C" Company.
5 "D" Company.
6 H.Q. [illegible].
7 [illegible].
8 Quartermaster.
9 Transport Officer.
10 Medical Officer.
11 [illegible].
12 [illegible] [illegible].

Copy No../3.....

OPERATION ORDERS NO. 54

by

Lieut. Colonel H.R. GADD M.C.,

Commanding,

2/5th. Battalion, The Sherwood Foresters.

.... 23.12.17.

Reference Map LENS 1/100,000

INTENTION 1. The Battalion will move to billets at HOUVIaN - HOUVIGNEUL as under :-
(a) Dismounted portion and a portion of 1st. Line Transport by train on 25th. instant.
(b) Remainder of 1st . Line Transport and baggage section by road on 24th. and 25th. instant.

TRAIN 2. Orders for move of sub para. (a) above will be issued ~~la~~ later.
The following transport will go by train :-
2 water carts
4 Field Kitchens
1 Maltese Cart
1 Mess Cart
1 Limbered G.S. Wagon for Lewis Guns.

TRANSPORT.3. The remainder of 1st, line Transport as in para. 1 (b) above, and loaded as detailed in para. 5,under, the Transport Officer will pass the road junction FAUBOURG-de - PERONNE at 8 a.m. tomorrow, and will bivouac for the night at ACHIET - LE - PETIT.
They will there come under orders of O.C. 59th. Divisional Train.
All wagons will be loaded by 12 midnight tonight. The Transp ort Officer will report when this is done.

BLANKETS. 4 There will be two lorries on 25th. instant to carry blankets and Officers' Kits.

LOADS. 5 The Transport proceeding by road will be loaded as follows :-
(a) Company Lewis Gun Wagons with complete loads less Lewis Guns and boxes, and four drums per gun. The Quartermaster will complete their loads with S.A.A. boxes.
(b) Tool wagons loaded complete less sufficient tools for sanitary purposes.
(c) Remainder of Limber wagons with Battalion S.A.A. Reserve.
(d) Two baggage wagons loaded with Quartermaster's Stores.

BILLETING PARTY. 6. 2nd. Lieut. C. WITT and 1 N.C.O . per Company and Headquarters will form billeting party and will proceed by lorry on 24th. instant. They will be at road junction BEAULENCOURT, N 18.a.2.0., at 8 a.m. They will carry one blanket per man and two days' rations.

7 ACKNOWLEDGE.

F.E. ANDREWS,
2nd. Lieutenant and Adjutant,

ISSUED AT p,m.

DISTRIBUTION.
1 Commanding Officer.
2 "A" Coy.
3 "B" Coy.
4 "C" Coy.
5 "D" Coy.
6 H.Q. Coy.
7 R.S.M.
8 2nd. Lieut. C. WITT
9 Medical Officer.
10. Quartermaster
11 Transport Officer
12 File abd Adjutant.
13 and 14 War diary

[illegible]

[illegible]

1\. [illegible] (a). [illegible]
(b). [illegible]

2\. [illegible]

3\. [illegible] (a). [illegible]
(b). [illegible]
(c). [illegible]

4\. [illegible]

[illegible signature]

[illegible]

ISSUED AT.........

DISTRIBUTION.

[illegible]

Adjutant

War Diary

OPERATION ORDERS No. 54. Copy 13.

by

Lieut. Colonel H.R.GADD M.C.

Commanding.

2/5th.Battalion, The Sherwood Foresters.

.... 24.12.17.

INSTRUCTIONS No 1.

1. INTENTION. The Battalion will move to-morrow in accordance with Operation Orders No. 54 para 1(a).

2. ENTRAINMENT.(a). The Battalion less Transport and "C" Company, will proceed by first train leaving BAPAUME at 9.30 a.m.

(b). "C" Company will proceed by second train leaving at 10 a.m. For the purposes of this "C" Coy. will be made up to 100 strong by attachment from Headquarters Coy.

(c) Transport as laid down in Operation Orders No 54 para, 2 will leave by train leaving BAPAUME at 10 a.m. Detraining Station - PETIT - HOUVIN.

3 (a) The Battalion less "C" Company will parade on Battalion Parade Ground ready to move off at 7 a.m.
DRESS - Marching Order over hairy coats.
(b) "C" Company will parade at BEAULENCOURT CAMP under Major OATES D.S.O., M.C., of the 2/8th. Sherwood Foresters, who will issue instructions as to times etc.
(c) Transport will be at BAPAUME STATION at 8 a.m., and will be under command of Major Oates D.S.O., M.C., who will issue orders to all concerned.

4. The 178th. M.G. Company and 17 men to be detailed by O.C. "C" Company, will be the loading and unloading party. O.C. "C" Company will ascertain when and where these men are to report.

5. 2nd. Lieut. H.E. Dickinson - mounted on a bicycle - will precede the column and warn all traffic controls of its approach. On arrival at BAPAUME STATION he will guide the Battalion to the Entraining Point.

6. On arrival in new area, the Quartermaster will send a representative to report to Town Major's Office, HOUVIN - HOUVIGNEUL, where a Supply detail of 516 Company A.S.C., will direct him to new Supply Re-filling Point.
Rations for consumption on the 26th. instant will be loaded up there on to train wagons.

7 Detail for Tomorrow.
Reveille 4.30 a.m. Breakfast 5.30 a.m.
All meat rations will be cooked today, and issued tonight for consumption tomorrow. All men will be warned that meat will not be consumed before dinner tomorrow. Tea will be cooked on the Field Kitchens, and will be issued on arrival in billets.
All water bottles will be filled by 8 p.m. tonight, and water for breakfast will be drawn by the same time.

8 Orders as to loading blankets, Officers' Kits and Mess Kits will be issued later.

9 ACKNOWLEDGE.

J.Andrews

2nd. Lieut. and Adjutant,

2/5th. Battalion, The Sherwood Foresters.

ISSUED AT 4.30 p.m.

DISTRIBUTION

NORMAL plus 178th. Infantry Brigade and Major Oates, 2/8th. Sherwood Foresters.

Confidential

Instructions regarding War Diaries and Intelligence Summaries are contained in F. S. Regs., Part II. and the Staff Manual respectively. Title Pages will be prepared in manuscript.

WAR DIARY
or
~~INTELLIGENCE SUMMARY~~
(Erase heading not required.)

2/5 Battn The Sherwood Foresters.

Vol 12

Army Form C. 2118.

Place	Date	Hour	Summary of Events and Information	Remarks and references to Appendices
[illegible]	1918 Jany 1		Company Training 1 Coy on fatigue clearing Bayonet Fighting Course.	
	2		Company Training Afternoon Inter Coy Football matches.	
	3		Company Training. " Running.	
	4		Coy Training under CSMs. Battn scheme for all Officers under Commanding Officer. Afternoon Football.	
	5		Platoon Training. Inspection of Battn in Saluting drill by CO ½ Battalion bathed.	
	6		Divine Services. Tactical Exercise under Bgde arrangements for CO. 2nd in C and Adjutant Rendez-vous Magnicourt 11 am	
	7		Coy training special attention to fitting equipment. Afternoon Football.	
	8		Inspection of Kit held. Lecture by CO to all Officers on Trench Routine. Lecture to Platoons on same subject.	
	9		Brigade run. Started from Billets 11 am. Battalion on fatigue clearing snow from Hersin – Fresnicourt Road.	
	10		Coy training. Tactical exercise for all Officers under CO 2.15 pm.	

2449 Wt. W14957/M90 750,000 1/16 J.B.C. & A. Forms/C.2118/12.

Confidential

Instructions regarding War Diaries and Intelligence Summaries are contained in F. S. Regs., Part II. and the Staff Manual respectively. Title Pages will be prepared in manuscript.

WAR DIARY
or
~~INTELLIGENCE SUMMARY~~
(Erase heading not required.)

2/5 Battn The Sherwood Foresters.

Army Form C. 2118.

Place	Date	Hour	Summary of Events and Information	Remarks and references to Appendices
Hornoy - Hornigneul.	Jany 11		Coy training. Football afternoon. Inspection of C & D Coys by CO.	JA
	12		½ Battn Bathed during day. Coy training. afternoon - Inter-platoon relay race. Coy training	JA
	13		Divine Services. Revolver Competition for all officers. Medical Insp. of Battn. by M.O.	JA
	14.		Company Training (Rapid deployment practice) Subaltern officers practice in message writing under Commanding Officer at 2.15 pm. Afternoon Football.	JA
	15		Brigade Field Day for officers, Platoon Sergeants and Lewis Gun NCOs. Inoculation of part of Battn. Remainder training under CSMs.	JA
	16		Company Training. Afternoon Football. 325 of Battn bathed.	JA
	17		Physical Training and Musketry. Platoons at disposal of Platoon Commanders. Tactical Exercise for all Subalterns and NCOs. 2pm. Rendezvous Map ref. 51C. 14.15 a 17.	JA
	18		Battalion Tactical Exercise in Training Area I 14. 19-20. Map 51C. Lecture on Fire Control at 5 15 pm	JA
	19		Company Training. Afternoon Football. Inspection by Divisional Commander of Battn by Companies and Transport.	JA

2449 Wt. W14957/M90 750,000 1/16 J.B.C. & A. Forms/C.2118/12.

Confidential

Instructions regarding War Diaries and Intelligence Summaries are contained in F. S. Regs., Part II. and the Staff Manual respectively. Title Pages will be prepared in manuscript.

WAR DIARY
or
~~INTELLIGENCE SUMMARY~~
(Erase heading not required.)

2/5 Battn The Sherwood Foresters.

Army Form C. 2118.

Place	Date	Hour	Summary of Events and Information	Remarks and references to Appendices
HOUVIN HOUVIGNEUL	Jany 20.		Divine Services. Part of Battn bathed.	
	21.		Companies at disposal of Coy Commanders for practice of Rapid Organization and launching Local Counter-attacks. Afternoon. Recreation Training under Coy arrangements. Tactical Scheme for officers 2.15 pm	
	22		Companies at disposal of Coy Commanders for practice of Rapid deployment. Recreational training.	
	23		Platoons at disposal of Platoon Commanders. Tactical Scheme for all Officers under CO & Major Trench at 2.15 pm	
	24		Company training. Recreational Training under Coy arrangements. Battn Fire Control Competition held (Eliminating Contest)	
	25		Battalion Tactical Exercise in Training Area I 14, 19 & 20 (Map 51C)	
	26		Companies at disposal of Coy Commanders. Recreational training under Coy arrangements during afternoon.	
	27		Divine Services. and Inspection of billets by Commanding Officer.	

2449 Wt. W14957/M90 750,000 1/16 J.B.C. & A. Forms/C.2118/12.

Confidential

Instructions regarding War Diaries and Intelligence Summaries are contained in F. S. Regs., Part II. and the Staff Manual respectively. Title Pages will be prepared in manuscript.

WAR DIARY
or
~~INTELLIGENCE SUMMARY~~
(Erase heading not required.)

2/5 Battn The Sherwood Foresters.

Army Form C. 2118.

Place	Date	Hour	Summary of Events and Information	Remarks and references to Appendices
Houvin-Houvigneul	Jany 28		Platoons at disposal of Platoon Commanders. Recreational training under Coy arrangements. Brigade Fire-Control competition.	[illegible]
	29		Platoon training. Cooperation of Sections practised. 25 men granted one days leave to Amiens	[illegible]
	30		Coy training. Arrival of draft from 2/8 Sherwood Foresters. Inspection of Spit Sets.	[illegible]
	31		Coys at disposal of Coy Commanders. Tactical Scheme for all Subalterns under CO at 2.15 pm. Recreational training.	[illegible]

[signature] Lt Col.
Comdg: 2/5 Notts & Derby Regt.

2449 Wt. W14957/M90 750,000 1/16 J.B.C. & A. Forms/C.2118/12.

Confidential

Instructions regarding War Diaries and Intelligence Summaries are contained in F. S. Regs., Part II. and the Staff Manual respectively. Title Pages will be prepared in manuscript.

2/5

WAR DIARY
or
INTELLIGENCE SUMMARY
(Erase heading not required.)

2/5 Battn The Sherwood Foresters.

Vol 13

Army Form C. 2118.

Place	Date 1918	Hour	Summary of Events and Information	Remarks and references to Appendices
HOUVIN HOUVIGNEUL	Feby 1		Coys at disposal of Coy Commanders. Boxing Competition held at 2.30 pm	
	2		Coys spent time Bombing. NCOs attended demonstration at Bde HQrs at 11 am. 325 Battalion bathed.	
	3		Divine Services. Foden Lorry used for fumigating blankets	
	4		Battalion Route March of about 8 miles. Afternoon - Recreational Training.	
	5		Coy training. Preparations for moving. Inspection of Bde by GOC VI Corps. Operation Orders for move to line issued	OO No 56
	6		Coy training. Platoons at disposal of Platoon Commanders. Btn Drill for one hour. Training of Platoon especially for Wiring.	
	7		Coys at disposal of Coy Commanders. Arrangements for moving made. Btn drill for 1 hour.	
	8		Bn left Houvin for BAVINCOURT.	

13-V

2449 Wt. W14957/M90 750,000 1/16 J.B.C. & A. Forms/C.2118/12.

Confidential

Instructions regarding War Diaries and Intelligence Summaries are contained in F. S. Regs., Part II. and the Staff Manual respectively. Title Pages will be prepared in manuscript.

WAR DIARY
or
INTELLIGENCE SUMMARY
(Erase heading not required.)

Army Form C. 2118.

2/5 Battn Sherwood Foresters

Place	Date 1918	Hour	Summary of Events and Information	Remarks and references to Appendices
BAVINCOURT	Feby 9.		Battn left BAVINCOURT for DURHAM CAMP BOISLEUX ST. MARC by march route	OO No 58
BOISLEUX ST MARC	10.		Left BOISLEUX - ST - MARC for MORY NORTH arrived about 2.10 pm. Draft of 38 o.r.s joined from 17th Battn.	OO. N. 59.
MORY.	11		Left MORY NORTH for line near BULLECOURT. Relieved 18th WELSH and 10/11 H.L.I. Relief complete by 9.50 pm.	~~OO No 60.~~
	12.		Two parties of 120 found by Battn for work: at 9 am and 5.31 pm.	
	13		Working Parties of 280 found by Battn for work.	
	14		Inter Coy. relief 2 Coys bathed at ST LEGER. Working Party of 4 Offrs and 246 supplied. Projector gas attack on Brigade front on our right. Front line heavily shelled from 8 - 9 pm and 10 - 11 pm.	OO No 60.
	15.		Working party of 230 supplied. Front line shelled from 6.30 - 7.30 am. Special Order re extra pay in line issued	OO No 61
	16		Working Party of 230 supplied. Quiet day in line.	

2449 Wt. W14957/M90 750,000 1/16 J.B.C. & A. Forms/C.2118/12.

Confidential

Instructions regarding War Diaries and Intelligence Summaries are contained in F. S. Regs., Part II. and the Staff Manual respectively. Title Pages will be prepared in manuscript.

WAR DIARY
or
INTELLIGENCE SUMMARY

(Erase heading not required.)

2/5 Battn The Sherwood Foresters

Army Form C. 2118.

Place	Date 1918	Hour	Summary of Events and Information	Remarks and references to Appendices
MORY	Feby 17		Battn relieved by 2/6 S.F. and went into Reserve at NORTH CAMP Mory.	O.O. No 62
	18		Battn kit inspection. Battalion bathed at MORY. Working party of 300 supplied for digging. Left Diamond Siding at 5 pm for NOREUIL. Emergency Orders in case of enemy attack issued.	
	19		Medical Inspection of Battn. Coys lectured by Coy Commanders for one hour on last tour in trenches.	
	20		Remainder of Battn bathed. Coy training carried out by Coys. Fatigue parties working on improvement of camp and Q.M. Stores. Lecture in the afternoon by OC Coys for one hour.	
	21		Working Party of 300 supplied as on 18th inst. at 5pm. Coy training except [illegible] on camp QM fatigues.	
	22		Fatigue for all men except 300 who were on Working Party previous night. Voluntary Coy [illegible] Service at Theatre Mory.	

2449 Wt. W14957/M90 750,000 1/16 J.B.C. & A. Forms/C.2118/12.

Confidential

Instructions regarding War Diaries and Intelligence Summaries are contained in F. S. Regs., Part II. and the Staff Manual respectively. Title Pages will be prepared in manuscript.

WAR DIARY
or
INTELLIGENCE SUMMARY
(Erase heading not required.)

2/5 Battn
The Sherwood Foresters.

Army Form C. 2118.

Place	Date	Hour	Summary of Events and Information	Remarks and references to Appendices
MORY	1918 Feb 23		Battn on fatigues during morning improving camps & Q M Stores - Transport Lines. Battn relieved 2/6 SF in left sub-sector of Brigade front. Relief complete by 9 45 pm. Battn foot inspection held before proceeding to line.	OO No. 63
	24		Working party of 210 men on trenches in Battn area. 2 Patrols sent out from right and left front Coys for reconnaissance.	
	25		Working party of 208 found by Battn on forward C T s and STRAY RESERVE trenches. Patrols sent out from right and left front Coys.	
	26		Working party of 210 found by Battn. 2 Patrols sent out from Battn front.	
	27		Working Party of 203 found by Battn 2 Patrols sent out from left front coys.	
	28		Working Party on Tyke Trench supplied. CO Adjt & Coy Commanders of 25 Northumberland Fusiliers reconnoitred line.	

R Chenevix Trench Major
Comd'g 2/5 Notts. & Derby Regt.

2449 Wt. W14957/M90 750,000 1/16 J.B.C. & A. Forms/C.2118/12.

SECRET. **OPERATION ORDERS.** No.56.

by

Lieut. Colonel H.R.Gadd M.C.

Commanding

2/5th. Battalion, The Sherwood Foresters.

5.2.18.

Reference Map :- CHERISY.Special Sheet. 1/10,000.

INTENTION. 1. The Battalion will take over the Trench Sector now held by Right Front Battalion of the 119th Infantry Brigade, near BULLECOURT, about the 10th inst.

DISPOSITION. 2. (a).The Front Line System will be held by 2 Companies,"B" on the Right, and "D" on the Left. These Companies will be based on the VALLEY SUPPORT LINE and will find Garrisons for the posts comprising the front line.
The dividing line in the Support Line will be U.20.d.8.4.
(b)."C" Company will be in Support and will be situated in MAN RESERVE.
(c)."A" Company will be in Reserve in RAILWAY RESERVE.
(d).Battalion Headquarters, Snipers and Wiring Platoon will be in RAILWAY RESERVE.

LEWIS GUNS. 3. The Front Line Companies will each have 2 Lewis Guns in the Line of Posts, and 2 in VALLEY SUPPORT.
There will be 1 Lewis Gun in each TRIDENT and VULCAN Posts.
Support and Reserve Companies will keep their Lewis Guns in hand.

SCHEME OF DEFENCE. 4. In case of Attack the Front Line posts and VALLEY SUPPORT will be held at all costs, and Companies in VALLEY SUPPORT will be prepared to form a Defensive Flank along PELICAN LANE and JOVE LANE.
The Support Company will be prepared to Counter Attack across the Open should the Enemy penetrate any portion of our line, and will also be prepared to form a defensive flank along QUEEN'S LANE should the Front of the Battalion on the Left be penetrated. This Company will Counter Attack without orders from Battalion Headquarters.
The Reserve Company will be prepared to Counter Attack across the Open and if necessary to form a Defensive Flank along PELICAN AVENUE.
A Determined Enemy advance must also be delayed by tenacious resistance in MAN and RAILWAY Reserves.

ADMINISTRATIVE ARRANGEMENTS. 5. (a).Front Line Companies will cook in VALLEY Support, and Support and Reserve Companies in RAILWAY Reserve.
(b).Water in TINS will be sent up with rations each night. By day it may be brought from ECOUST.
(c).A sock drying room will be established near Battalion Headquarters, Dry socks will be issued from here and NOT from the Q.M. Stores.
(d).Whale Oil will be drawn from R.A.P. daily.

DRESS. 6. Hairy and Great Coats will be taken into Trenches.
Haversacks will not be taken, but will be left at Q.M.Stores filled with spare kit.

R. A. P. 7. The R.A.P. will be in RAILWAY Reserve.

8. A C K N O W L E D G E .

ISSUED AT..........

H. Andrews.
Captain and Adjutant.

DISTRIBUTION.

No. 1. Commanding Officer.
2. 2nd.in Command.
3. Adjutant.
4. Quartermaster.
5. Transport Officer.
6. Medical Officer.
7. R.S.M.

No. 8. "A" Company.
9. "B" "
10. "C" "
11. "D" "
12. H.Q. "
13. File.
14 & 15. War Diary.

OPERATION ORDERS No 57

No 14

by

Lieut. Colonel H. [illegible] M.C.

Commanding

2/5th Battalion. Sherwood Foresters.

7.2.18.

Reference Map. Lens 11- 1/100,000

1. INTENTION. The Battalion will march tomorrow to BAVINCOURT.

2. PARADE & DRESS. The Battalion less Transport will parade in Column of Route on HOUVIN-STREE WAMIN Road with head of Column at Cross Roads by "B" Company's Billet (No 6) ready to move off at 9.35 a.m.

Order of March. Headquarters. "B" "D" Drums "A" "C".

DRESS. Marching Order- Hairy Coats will be carried under Supporting Straps of the pack.

ROUTE. ETIJE [illegible] WAMIN- LE COUROY - LIENCOURT-GRAND RULLECOURT-SOMBRIN-SAULTY- Destination.

The Transport will Parade on road by Quartermasters Stores with head of Transport also by "B" Company's Billet ready to move off at 9.35 a.m.
Transport will march immediately in rear of the Battalion. 300 yards interval will be maintained between head of Battalion and rear of Transport in front.

3. BILLETING PARTY. A Billeting Party consisting of 2nd. Lieut. H.D. BARROWS and 1 N.C.O. per Company will report at Brigade Headquarters at 6.50 a.m. tomorrow, where a lorry will convey them to new area. Each N.C.O. will be in possession of billeting strength of Officers and Other Ranks in his Company.
On arrival at BAVINCOURT, the party will report at the Town Major's Office. The officer in charge of party will arrange to have a guide to meet Battalion on SAULTY - BAVINCOURT ROAD.

.TRANSPORT. Supply and Baggage Wagons (plus one extra G.S. wagon) will report at Quartermaster's Stores at 4 p.m. today. These wagons will march with Battalion transport. Supply Wagons will be returned to 516 Coy, A.S.C. immediately rations are off-loaded.

Baggage wagon plus extra G.S. Wagon will remain with Battalion until completion of move.
Three lorries will be provided and the Quartermaster will arrange for a guide to be at Brigade Headquarters at 8 a.m. tomorrow. Lorries will be returned on completion of day's move.

.KITS (a) Blankets will be tightly rolled in bundles of 10, tied in three places, labelled and dumped at "Crumps" Hall by 8 a.m. tomorrow.
(b) Officers' Kits. All Officers' valises will be dumped at "Crumps" Hall by 8.30 a.m. tomorrow. The Orderly Officer will superintend the dumping of blankets and valises at the Hall.
(c) Mess Boxes. The Company Mess Boxes will be ready for collection at 8.45 a.m. The Mess Cart will collect in order :- " C", "D", "A", "B", H.Q.
(d) 100 lbs. extra stores per Company.
The 100 lbs. extra stores allowed per Company will be dumped at Quartermaster's Stores tonight.
(e) The rifles and packs of the Band will be dumped at " Crumps" Hall by 8 a.m. tomorrow.
One Officer per Company will be detailed at see that all stores mentioned in sub paras. (a),(b),(c),(d) and (e) are ready at the times specified.

6. SLOW PARTY.. A slow party under 2nd. Lieut L. J. de Mauny will parade outside Battalion Orderly Room at same time as Battalion. Companies will detail men for this party whom they do not consider capable of completing the march with Battalion. Names will be rendered to Battalion Orderly Room by 8 p.m. tonight. No man will be allowed to fall out from the Column without written permission from an Officer. Any man so falling out will wait on right of road for Slow party and will complete march with them. The names of of all men falling out will be reported to Adjutant immediately after arrival in New area.

7. BILLETS. All billets will be left clean and tidy and ready for inspection by Commanding Officer at 9 a.m.

8. TRAINING STORES. (a) All surplus R.E. Material will be handed in to Quarter-Masters Stores tonight. This material will be handed over to incoming Unit.
(b). "Blob Sticks" received whilst here will be handed over to incoming Unit. Any Sticks in possession of Companies will be dumped at Quartermaster Stores.

9. LEWIS GUNS. Lewis Gun Limbers will report to Company Report Centres tonight.

10. WATERING. During the march horses will be watered from tins carried on the Transport.

11. A C K N O W L E D G E.

ISSUED AT..3-0......p.m.

DISTRIBUTION.

J.E. Andrews.
Captain ~~and~~ Adjutant.

Copy No 1. Commanding Officer.
2. 2nd in Command.
3. Adjutant.
4. Quartermaster.
5. Transport Officer.
6. Medical Officer.
7. R.S.M.
8. "A" Company.
9. "B" "
10. "C" "
11. "D" "
12. H.Q. "
13. File.
14.)
15.) War Diary.
16. 2nd.Lieut M.D.Barrows.
17. Orderly Officer.
18. 2nd.Lieut R.Stone.

OPERATION ORDERS No. 58 Copy No....14.

by

Lt. Colonel H.R. GADD M.C.,

Commanding

2/5th. Battalion, The Sherwood Foresters

.... 8.2.1918.

Reference Map 51 b 1/40,000 and LENS 11 1/100,000

1. The Battalion will move by route march to DURHAM CAMP, BOISLEUX - St. MARK tomorrow. Time and position of paradr will be notified later.

2. The Battalion will march with intervals of 200 yards between Companies. Transport will march 200 yards in rear of Battalion. An interval of 300 yards will be maintained between head of Battalion, and rear of transport of Unit in front.

3 The route will be Cross roads N.W. of 1st. R in RIVIERE - BRETENCOURT - BLAIRVILLE - FICHEUX - Destination.

4. Orders for loading blankets etc will be issued later.

5. All transport will be parked at M 16 d.

6. No man will be allowed to fall out without permission of an Officer in writing and any man so doing will wait for slow party. The Slow Party will be in charge of Orderly Officer and will parade in accordance with instructions to be issued. Companies will detail men for this party who they do not consider will be able to complete march with Battalion.

7. All billets and area will be left tidy.

8. A Billeting Party under 2nd. Lieut. M.D. Barrows will be detailed. Full particulars will be issued as soon as known.

9. ACKNOWLEDGE.

J.E. Andrew.

Captain and Adjutant,

2/5th. Battalion, The Sherwood Foresters.

DISTRIBUTION.

Copy No. 1. Commanding Officer.
2 Second in Command
3 Adjutant
4 Quartermaster
5 Transport Officer
6 Medical Officer
7 "A" Coy.
8 "B" Coy.
9 "C" Coy.
10 "D" Coy.
11 Headquarters
12 R.S.M.
13 File
14 & 15 War Diary.
16 2nd. Lieut. Barrows.
17 Orderly Officer.

Copy No.......14

OPERATION ORDERS No 58.
by
Lieut. Colonel H.R.Gadd M.C.
Commanding
2/5th. Battalion, The Sherwood Foresters.

8.2.18.

War Diary

INSTRUCTIONS No. 1.

Reference Maps LENS II, & FRANCE 51.b.

1. The Battalion will parade in column of route on the BAVINCOURT-LA CAUCHIE Road ready to move off at 10.40 a.m. tomorrow.
Order of March :- H.Q, "D", "A", Drums, "B", "C".
The head of the column will be level with present position of "A","B" & "D" Companies' Cookers. The Transport will be formed up and will move off from present position of G.S. Limbers by Transport Lines.

2. KITS Etc.
(a). BLANKETS. will be tightly rolled in bundles of 10, tied in three places, labelled and dumped at Quartermaster's Stores by 8.30 a.m.
(b). OFFICER'S KITS. All Officer's Valises will be dumped at Q.M. Stores by 9.30 a.m.
(c). MESS BOXES. Company Mess Boxes will be ready for collection at 9.30 a.m. The Mess cart will collect in the following order :- "D", "H.Q", "C", "B", "A".
(d). 100LBS EXTRA COMPANY STORES. The extra 100 lbs allowed per Coy. will be dumped at Q.M. Stores by 8.30 a.m.
(e). THE RIFLES AND PACKS OF THE "DRUMS". will be at Q.M. Stores by 8.30 a.m.
One Officer per Company will be detailed, and will be held responsible for seeing that stores as specified in sub. paras. A,B,C & D. are ready punctually at times specified.

3. SLOW PARTY.
A Slow Party under the Orderly Officer will parade outside Battalion Orderly Room at 10.30 a.m. ready to move off at same time as Battalion. Men whose names were handed in on "Returns" parade today will be ordered to parade. On arrival in New area the Orderly Officer will report to Adjutant.

4. RATIONS.
Haversack Rations will be carried.

5. TRANSPORT.
The Quartermaster will be notified in regard to lorries and guides for same as soon as particulars are available.

6. BILLETING.
Companies will detail 1 N.C.O. each who will be in possession of usual billeting particulars to form billeting party for Battalion.
Time and position of parade will be notified.

7. A C K N O W L E D G E.

ISSUED AT.. 10.15 pm

Captain and Adjutant.

DISTRIBUTION.

Copy No
1. Commanding Officer.
2. 2nd in Command.
3. Adjutant.
4. Quartermaster.
5. Transport Officer.
6. Medical Officer.
7. "A" Company.
8. "B" "
9. "C" "
10. "D" "
11. H.Q. "
12. R.S.M.
13. File.

No 14.)
15.) War Diary.
16. 2nd.Lieut. M.D. Barrows.
17. Orderly Officer.

SECRET OPERATION ORDERS No. 59 Copy No. 14.

by

Lieut. Colonel H.R. GADD M.C.,

Commanding

2/5th. Battalion, The Sherwood Foresters.

War Diary

....

9.2.1918.

Reference Maps LENS 11 and FRANCE 51b 1/40,000

1. INTENTION The Battalion will proceed by route march to MORY NORTH, tomorrow 10th. instant, and will relieve the 12th. S.W. Borders.

2. PARADE AND DRESS (a) The Battalion will parade in Mass on ground, West side of Huts, ready to move off at 9.30 a.m. Headquarters Coy. including the Drums will parade on right flank of Battalion, and will move off with leading Company. Companies will maintain 200 yards interval, and Transport with Battalion will march 200 yards in rear of last Company.
(b) DRESS Marching Order - Hairy coats will be carried under supporting straps of pack.
(c) ROUTE BOYELLES - ERVILLERS - Destination.
(d) Company Cookers, Lewis Gun Limbers, Mess Cart, Valise Wagon and Maltese Cart will parade on road leading from Camp to BOISLEUX St. MARC - BOIRY-BECQUERELLE Road, at same time a Battalion.

3. BILLETING PARTY. An Advance Party consisting of 2nd. Lieut. M.D. BARROWS, and 1 N.C.O. per Company will precede the Battalion. N.C.O's detailed will be warned to parade by Battalion Orderly Room at time to be notified.

4. TRANSPORT Two lorries will report at Camp at 8 a.m. Each of these lorries will perform two journeys. The Quartermaster will arrange the loads, and will detail a guide to meet lorrie when they arrive at DURHAM CAMP.
The Transport Officer will arrange for valise wagons, Mess Cart and Maltese Cart to be at Camp at 8.30 a.m. punctually and Officers' Chagers to be at Camp by 9 a.m.

5. KITS (a) Blankets will be tightly rolled in tens, labelled and dumped at entrance to Camp by 8 a.m.
(b) Officers' kit. All Officers' valises will be dumped at entrance to Camp by 8.30 a.m.
(c) Mess Boxes. All Company Mess Boxes will be ready for collection punctually at 8.45 a.m. The Mess Cart will report at end of duck board track, leading to Mess Hut at this time.
(d) 100 lbs. extra Stores per Companywill be dumped at entrance to Camp a 8.30 a.m.
(e) The Rifles and packsof the Band will be dumped at entrance to Camp by 8.15 a.m.
(f) R.A.P. Stores will be collected at 8.45 a.m.
The Orderly Officer willsuperintend the dumping of all stores, and O.C. "A" Company will arrange to detail 1 N.C.O. and 3 men (three) as guard over the dump. Each Company willdetail an Officer to be responsible for punctual dumping of all stores.

6. SLOW PARTY A Slow Party under the Orderly Officer will parade on left flank of Battalion. Names of men detailed for this party will be sent to Orderly Room by 8 a.m. tomorrow. The names of all men falling out from Battalion will be reported to Adjutant immediately on arrival in new area.

7. CAMP. All huts and area will be left clean and tidy.

8. ACKNOWLEDGE.

G. Andrews
Captain and Adjutant,
2/5th. Battalion, The Sherwood Foresters.

ISSUED AT p.m.

DISTRIBUTION.

Copy No.		Copy No.	
1	Commanding Officer	2	2nd. in Command.
3	Adjutant	4	Quartermaster
5	Transport Officer	6	Medical Officer.
7	"A" Coy.	8	"B" Coy.
9	"C" Coy.	10	"D" Coy.
11	Headquarters Coy.	12	R.S.M.
13	File	14 & 15	War Diary
16	2nd. Lieut. M.D. Barrows	17	Orderly Officer.

SECRET. OPERATION ORDERS No 36. Copy No. 17

by

Lieut. Colonel H.R.Gadd M.C.
Commanding
2/5th. Battalion, The Sherwood Foresters.

10.2.18.

INSTRUCTIONS No 1.

RELIEF. The Relief will take place tomorrow 11th inst, and will be divided into 2 parts.
(a). "A" & "C" Companies will relieve 18th Welsh Regiment.
(b). Battalion Headquarters, "B" & "D" Companies will relieve 10/11 Battalion H.L.I.

GUIDES FOR RELIEF (a). Relief (a) will take place by daylight, Companies moving off from present Camp as follows :- "C" Coy. 10.15 a.m.,
"A" Coy. 10.35 a.m.
Route:- St LEGER, CROISILLES.
Guides:- One per platoon will join Companies tonight.
On arrival in trenches, these Companies will come under command of Lt.Colonel. Hodgkin D.S.O. until the arrival of Battalion Headquarters after dark.

GUIDES FOR RELIEF. (b). Relief (b) will take place after dark.
Companies will move off from present Camp as under :-
"B" Company - 4.30 p.m. "D" Company - 4.40 p.m. H.Q. 4.50 pm
GUIDES One per company and One for Headquarters will be at Brigade Headquarters, L'Homme Mort at 5.30 p.m. and will conduct Companies to "RAILWAY RESERVE" where post guides will become available. Companies will move off from this Camp with their POSTS organised in the proper order.

INTERVALS. Movements in the case of (a) will be by half platoons, with platoons at 3 minutes interval, and in the case of (b) by Platoons at 100 yards interval.

TRANSPORT. Each Company will be allotted One Limber Wagon, and Headqrs Two Limbers - for Lewis Gunsetc; and One Limber for Every two Companies for Cooking Utensils, these will report at present camp as under :-
"A" & "C" Companies ------- 8.30 a.m.
H.Q. "B" & "D" Coys ------- 3.30 p.m.

STORES, KITS ETC. (a). All blankets will be handed in to representative of Q.M. at this Camp at 8.30 a.m.
(b). Surplus Officers Kits and surplus mens kits(in haversacks) of "A" & "C" Companies will be handed in to representative of Quartermaster by 9.30 a.m.
(c)Surplus Officers Kits and mens kits(in haversacks) of remainder of Battalion will be handed to representative of Q.M. by 3 p.m.
(d). The mess cart will leave MORY Camp at 4.30 p.m. with all mess goods not required in the Line.

PERSONNEL. The following will remain at Quartermaster 's Stores in addition to Transport and Q.M. Stores personnel :-
All pool officers
Drums
Any cooks in excess of 3 per Company.
Company Quartermaster Sergeants.
Orderly Room Sergeant.
2nd.Lieut. L.J. de Mauny will be in charge of these details.

COMPULSORY GARRISONS FOR ATTACK. Compulsory Garrisons as under will be found by Companies as detailed below, in case of attack:-

STRENGTH	POSITION	FOUND BY
1 platoon) 1 Lewis Gun)	MAIN RESERVE	Support Company.
1 Lewis Gun	U.20.c.7.9.	
1 Platoon	No 15 post. Railway Reserve U.26.c.2.6.	Reserve Company.
1 Platoon	No 14 post. Railway Reserve U.26.c.0.8.	Reserve Company.

SECRET. OPERATION ORDERS No 56. Copy No.........12

by

Lieut. Colonel H.R. Gadd M.C.

Commanding

2/5th. Battalion, The Sherwood Foresters.

10.2.18.

ADMINISTRATIVE INSTRUCTIONS No 2.

RATIONS. Rations will be brought by DECAUVILLE to Divisional Siding in B.14.d. They are then prepared for the Line by the Q.M. in the Hut built at the siding, and are again loaded in the train which proceeds at dusk to GUINNESS Dump, N.W. of ECOUST. They are then transferred to the light railway and pushed by hand to Battalion Headquarters.
The Reserve Company will detail 15 men to push ration trucks and to be at GUINNESS Dump at 5.30 p.m. Daily. Company Ration Carrying Parties will be at Battalion Headquarters at 6.30 p.m. Daily.

WATER. Water will be drawn from point at St LEGER and brought up to be at Battalion Headquarters at following times daily:-
9 a.m. 2 p.m. 5 p.m.
Petrol Cans will be filled from Water Carts and drawn from the R.S.M. for filling water bottles at 6.30 p.m. nightly.
The water carts willremain for the night at St. LEGER under the supervision of Water Duty men, who will billet there.
Horses will return to ERVILLERS.

SALVAGE The following arra ngement for salvage will be practised :- Companies will collect salvage and hand it over to Reserve Company by 3 p.m. daily. The party as detailed in para . 1 will carry it to GUINNES DUMP, and hand it over to two salvage men detailed by the Quartermaster, who will come up with the ration train. The Quartermaster will arrange to deliver it to Divisional Salvage Dump. ERVILLERS.

BURIALS All bodies will be sent direct to ST LEGER Graveyard by the Company concerned.

FOOT TREATMENT Before leaving here all men will rub their feet with whale-oil. The Quartermaster will issue all whale-oil to the Medical Officer, and Companies will draw their daily requirements from the R.A.P. They will bring a receptacle with them.

GUM BOOTS The R.S.M. will take over the Battalion Gum Boot Stores from the 10/11 H.L.I., and the 18th. Welsh Regiment. Storemen will be detailed in charge of each.

R.E.WORKING PARTY The following Permanent R.E. working party will report at GUINNES DUMP at 3 p.m. 11th. instant.
2nd. Lieut. H.C. Pickthall and "A" Coy. 7 Other Ranks
"B" Coy. 8 Other Ranks "C" Coy. 7 Other Ranks "D" 8 O.R's.
The Quartermaster will send rations for the party with the Unit's rations as far as Guinnes Dump. 2nd. Lieut. Pickthall will get into touch with the R.E's at ECOUSTE tomorrow morning.

SOUP KITCHEN A Brigade Soup Kitchen exists at "RAILWAY RESERVE". The Rev'd. Smith Masters will be in charge. Private Goodwine (Cook) will report forduty to him at 11 a.m. tomorrow at Brigade Headquarters. He will be rationed by the 178th. T.M.B. The Quartermaster will indent for the full amount of preserved rations, and delived he surplus to the Brigade Soup Kitchen.

RECEIPTS Receipts for all stores taken over by Companies - including Tracer and Armour piercing S.A.A. - will reach Battalion Headquarters by 12 noon on the 12th instant.

10. SOCKS Sub para. (c) of para. 5 Operation Orders No. 56 is cancelled. The Quartermaster will send up to Battalion Headquarters each day by 3 p.m. 500 dry pairs of socks. These will be handed over to Lce. Corpl. Lewendon. Companies will send down all wet socks by 8 p.m. nightly, and will draw an equal number of dry socks from Lce. Corpl. Lewendon. Any surplus dry socks will be retained by him as a reserve.

11. ACKNOWLEDGE.

J.E. Andrews.
Captain and Adjutant,
2/5th. Battalion, The Sherwood Foresters.

ISSUED AT p.m.
DISTRIBUTION.

Copy No.		Copy No.	
1	Commanding Officer	2	2nd. in Command
3	Adjutant	4	O.C. "A" Coy.
5	O.C. "B" Coy.	6	O.C. "C" Coy.
7	O.C. "D" Coy.	8	Headquarters Coy.
9	Quartermaster	10	Transport Officer
11	R.S.M.	12 and 13	War Diary
14	File	15	Medical Officer.

Secret. Operation Orders No 60. Copy No 8.

by

Lieut. Colonel. H.R. Gadd. M.C.

Commanding

2/5th Battalion. Sherwood Foresters.

13-2-18.

1. An Inter-Coy Relief will be carried out in the Battalion Sector tomorrow.

2. Front Line Companies will be relieved as under:

   "A" Coy will relieve "B" Coy

   "C" " " " "D" Coy.

3. OC's "A" & "C" Coys will visit O.C "B" & "D" Coys respectively and make all necessary arrangements for relief to be carried out. Arrangements will be so made that the relief of all men in VALLEY SUPPORT Line is complete by 4 pm. The relief of posts comprising the Front Line will be carried out as soon after dark as possible.
   After Relief "B" Coy will be Reserve Coy in RAILWAY RESERVE and "D" Coy will be Support Coy in MAN Reserve.

4. The present Officers in charge of Front Line Coys will remain in charge of composite Coys after relief of VALLEY SUPPORT until the whole relief of their Coys is complete.

5. Companies will move off from their present positions tomorrow night with their posts organised in the proper order.

6. Patrolling at night will be carried out as usual by each Front Line Coy. The outgoing Company will be responsible for this being done but a proportion of the composition of the patrol will be supplied by the incoming Company.

7. Completion of Relief will be notified to Battn Hd Qrs by Code Word "ARMY BEER"

8. ACKNOWLEDGE.

Issued At. 11.15 pm

DISTRIBUTION.

1. Commanding Officer. 2. "A" Coy.
3. "B" Coy. 4. "C" Coy.
5. "D" Coy. 6. Adjt & File.
7 & 8. War Diary 9. 2/6 S. Fors. 10. 178th Inf Bde.

[signature] Capt. and Adjt.
2/5 Notts. & Derby Regt.

War Diary

ORDERS No 61.

1. The Left Front Company will by night establish a Lewis Gun Post at the bottom of the valley by junction of GOLLYWOG LANE and the front line, by day this gun will be in No 7 Post.

2. By day "A" Coy will establish a Lewis Gun Post in VALLEY SUPPORT about U 20 d. 73. 88 from where it can command the valley running N.E.
The exact position will be reconnoitred by the Lewis Gun Officer and the Map Reference reported.

3. The dividing line between Companies in VALLEY SUPPORT will be U 20 d. 60. 75.

E. Andrews Capt. and Adjt.
2/5 Notts. & Derby Regt.

2/5th. Battalion, The Sherwood Foresters.

D E F E N C E S C H E M E

RIGHT SUB-SECTOR

In continuation and supercession of Operation Order No. 56 para. [illegible], and Instructions No. 1 para. 2.

DISPOSITION 1. (a) The Front Line System consists of VALLEY SUPPORT TRENCH covered by a line of 12 posts about 300 yards in advance. The Posts are numbered from Right to Left commencing with No. 1.

The Front Line System is sub-divided into two sectors, each held by a Company.

(b) The Support Company is located in MAN Reserve,

(c) The Reserve Company and Battalion Headquarters are located in RAILWAY RESERVE, about U 26.c.2.6.

ACTION IN CASE OF ATTACK. 2. In case of attack the Battalion may be considered under two headings :-

(a) Garrisons of certain lines and localities which must be held at all costs, no matter what the situation is, or to what depth the enemy has penetrated.

(b) Counter-attack formations which are used either for instant counter-attack on the initiative of their immediate Commanders, or for a more premeditated attack under orders of the Battalion Commander.

GARRISONS 3. The following will be held at all costs in accordance with para. 2 (a) above :-

LOCALITY	GARRISON	STRENGTH
Line of Posts) VALLEY SUPPORT)	Right and Left Front Companies.	2 Companies.
MAN RESERVE	Support Company	1 Platoon 1 Lewis Gun
U 20.c.7.9.	Support Company	1 Lewis Gun.
No. 13 Post) RAILWAY RESERVE) U 26.c.2.6.)	Reserve Company	1. Platoon
No. 14 Post) RAILWAY RESERVE) U 26.c.0.8.)	Wiring Platoon	1 Officer and 36 men.

COUNTER-ATTACK. FORMATIONS The forces available for counter-attack will therefore be:-

(a) 3 Platoons less 1 Lewis Gun Section of the Support Company.

(b) 3 Platoons of the Reserve Company.

Of the above (a) will be for immediate counter-attack on the initiative of the Company Commander, whilst (b) will only act under the orders of the Battalion Commander.

DEFENSIVE FLANKS 5. AND SWITCHES Should any portion of the Front be penetrated, the Commander on the spot will immediately attempt to localize the enemy's success by forming a defensive flank, and manning the Switch Lines.

It is impossible to lay down definitely what troops would be available for this duty, but they should, if possible, be taken from the garrisons, thus leaving as many as possible of the counter-attack formations available for their allotted functions. It may, however, be necessary to utilize counter-attack troops for this, and the Officers Commanding Support and Reserve Companies will make themselves acquainted with the Flank Defences and Switch Lines they may have to man.

The most likely lines in this case are PELICAN LANE and PELICAN AVENUE on the right, and JOVE LANE and QUEEN'S LANE on the left.

ANTI-TANK DEFENCES 6. In the event of an attack by hostile Tanks, arrangements have been made for dealing with the Tanks with our Artillery, and our rifle and Lewis Gun fire should be directed at the enemy's Infantry, which would be following to make good the ground gained. Lewis Guns in VALLEY SUPPORT have been issued with Armour piecing S.A.A., which should be used should the Tanks reach short range.

ANTI-AIRCRAFT DEFENCES. 7. Anti-Aircraft Lewis Guns will be mounted as under :-

LOCALITY	BY WHOM FOUND
Battalion Headquarters	Reserve Company.
MAN Reserve	Support Company.
VALLEY SUPPORT (2)	Front Line Companies.

All these guns are available in the case of an Infantry attack.

Lieut.-Colonel,

15.2.1918. Commanding, 2/5th. Battalion, Sherwood Foresters.

DISTRIBUTION

Copy No. 1 Commanding Officer.
2 2nd. in Command
3 2nd. Lieut. R. Stone
4 O.C. "A" Coy.
5 O.C. "B" Coy.
6 O.C. "C" Coy.
7 O.C. "D" Coy.
8 O.C. H.Qrs. Coy.
9 2/6th. Bn., S.F.
10 178th. Infantry Brigade.
11 2/5th. Lincolns
12. Copy to hand over to Relieving Battalion.
13 File
14 & 15 War Diary.

SECRET. OPERATION ORDERS No 62 Copy No....11....

by

Lieut. Colonel. H.R.GADD. M.C.

Commanding

2/5th Battalion Sherwood Foresters.

.... 16.2.18.

1.INTENTION. The battalion will be relieved by the 7th Battalion Sherwood Foresters.

2.TIME. The relief will take place after dusk.

3 ORDER OF RELIEF.

Companies will berelieved in the following order :-
"A" "C" "B" "D" by the corresponding Companies of the 7th Battalion.

4.GUIDES. Guides as under will be supplied :-

(a) 1 Guide per Company and 1 for Battalion Headquarters will be at Brigade Headquarters at 5.30 p.m. These will be found by the Battalion Snipers.

(b) 1 Guide per Post and 1 for the remainder of Company will be sent by each front line Company ("A & "C") to Battalion Headquarters in RAILWAY RESERVE by 5.30 p.m.

(c) 1 Guide per Platoon for "D" Company will alsobe at Battalion Headquarters RAILWAY RESERVE at 5.30 p.m.

Guides as per (b) & (c) will report to 2nd Lieut.A.O.Robinson at time stated.They will each come provided with a piece of paper showing No Of Post or Platoon thay are Guiding to.

5.BILLETING PARTY. (a) A Billeting Party from incoming Battalion will report at Battalion Headquarters at 3 p.m. today. They will allot available accommodation in RAILWAY RESERVE to their Headquarte and Reserve Companies. 2nd Lieut. G.Manning will show this party all available accommodation.

(b) 1 N.C.O. and 2 Men per Company (including Officers Mess) and 1 N.C.O. from Headquarters will report to 2nd Lieut M.D.Barrows at Battalion Headquarters at 2. p.m. They will proceed to MORY Camp North and allot accommodation.

6 TRANSPORT. Transport is allotted as follows :-

Each Company for Lewis Guns, Officers Kits etc-1 Lim Wagon
Each Company for Cooking Utensils etc- ½ " "
Headquarters Company. 1 " "

All the above will be junction of HOGS BACK and RAILWAY RESERVE at 7 p.m.

Headquarters Company, Officers Kits, Canteen and availabl Signalling Stores. 1 Limber Wagon.

to be at same place at 6 p.m.

Headquarters Company for Officers Mess and any surplus Kit... 1 Limber Wagon.

To be at same placeeat 8.30 p.m.

The R.S.M. will be responsible for allotting and the leading of all the above wagons excepting the last named. Companies should send down as much Kit as early as possible before the relief commences. This will be handed over to the R.S.M.

7 WATER TINS. All Wtare Tins other than the 40 handed over at Battalion Headquarters by the 10/11 H.L.I. will be taken out. As many as possible will be loaded on the crate of the water carts and the remainder distributed by the R.S.M. among the limbered wagons. All water cans will be returned to the R.S.M. by 5 p.m. to-day.

8. ADVANCE PARTIES. (a) 1 man per L.G.Team of the 7th Battn: will arrive during the afternoon. Each Company will have a guide at 2.30 p.m. at Battn Hdqrs to take these men to Coy: Hdqrs.
(b) A Warrant Officer or N.C.O. for each Company Hdqrs will accompany the L.G.party.
(c) The Battn. Gas N.C.O. will meet the Battn. Gas N.C.O. of the 7th. S.F. at Battn. Hdqrs at 3 p.m. and hand over all Gas appliances.

9. TRENCH STORES. All Trench Stores will be handed over and a receipt sent to Battn. Hdqrs by 12 noon to-morrow (18th inst.) A separate receipt will be obtained for the Armour Piercing Ammunition.

10. PERSONNEL. All those detailed in O.O. 59 Instructions No.1. para 7. will join the Battalion to-morrow morning by 11 a.m. In addition Tailors and Shoemakers will be accommodated at MORY CAMP.

11. ANTI AIRCRAFT GUARDS. On arrival in Camp "B" Coy: will at once send 3 Lewis Guns and teams for the Anti-Aircraft protection of Transport as under :-

1 Gun :- 2/5th & 2/8th S.F.Lines at BELFAST and ENNISKILLING Camp at ERVILLERS.
1 Gun :- 7th S.F.Lines at ARMAGH Camp No.2. HAMELINCOUR.
1 Gun :- 2/6th Lines CLONNEL Camp HAMELINCOURT.

"B" Company will retain a limbered wagon to take the Guns to these Camps and the Transport Officer will provide a Driver who knows their position.

12. STORE KITS. The following articles will be issued to Companies to-night :-

Blankets.
Officers' Kits.
Officers' Mess Boxes.

and the following will be issued to-morrow morning :-

Haversacks.

13. ACKNOWLEDGE.

Issued at ...... p.m.
Distribution :-
1. C.O.
2. 2nd in-Command.
3. Adjutant & File.
4. "A" Coy%
6. "B" "
6. "C" "
7. "D" Coy
8. "H.Q"s.
9. 7th S.F.
10. 178th Inf. Bde.
11.)
12.) War Diary.

War Diary

OPERATION ORDERS No. 63. Copy No. 13

- by -

MAJOR C.R.C. Trench

Commanding

2/5th Bn SHERWOOD FORESTERS. 22.2.1918.

Reference Map CHERISY
Special Sheet, 1/10,000.

1. INTENTION. The Battalion will relieve the 2/6th Bn Sherwood Foresters on the night of the 23/24th February.

2. DISPOSITIONS. (a) The Front line system will be held by 2 Companies "D" on the Right, "B" on the left. These Companies will find garrisons for the posts comprising the front line.
The dividing line between the front line Coys: will be KNUCKLE AVENUE.
(b) "A" Company will be in Support and will be situated in STRAY RESERVE.
(c) "C" Company will be in Reserve in RAILWAY RESERVE.
(d) Battalion Headquarters will be in RAILWAY RESERVE. The Signal Section will take over the position as at present occupied by the 2/6th Sherwood Foresters.
(e) The Wiring Platoon will be accommodated by the Reserve Company.

3. LEWIS GUNS. Lewis Gun positions will be taken over as at present.

4. SCHEME OF DEFENCE. In case of attack the Front Line Posts and DURY Support to be held at all costs. The Right Front Company will be prepared to form a Defensive Flank down MARS LANE and QUEENS LANE, and the Left Front Company down HUMP LANE and HUMP SUPPORT.
The Support Company will be prepared to counterattack across the open should the enemy penetrate any portion of our line. This Company will act without ordersfrom Battn. Hdqrs.
The Reserve Company will act only under orders from Battn. Hdqrs.

5. R.A.P. The R.A.P. will be at THE KNUCKLE.

6. DRESS. Hairy and Great Coats will be taken into the Trenches. Haversacks will not be taken into the ~~Front~~ Line but will be left at Quartermaster's Stores under arrangements to be notified later.

7. COMPLETION OF RELIEF. Completion of Relief will be reported by code words as follows :-
"A" Coy :- MABEL. "B" Coy:- "INTERPRETER".
"C" Coy:- "SOAP SUDS"
"D" Coy :- "QUEENIE".

8. ACKNOWLEDGE.

[signature]
Captain & Adjutant.

Issued at 2-10 pm

Distribution :-

1. Commanding Officer.	2. 2nd in Command.
3. Adjutant.	4. "A" Coy.
5. "B" Coy:	6. "C" Coy:
7. "D" Coy:	8. "HQs" Coy:
9. Medical Officer.	10. Q.M.
11. R.S.M.	12 & 13 War Diary.
14. File.	15. 2/6th S.F.
16. 178th Inf. Brigade.	

9. WIRING PLATOON. The wiring platoon will tomorrow join "A" Company and will be attached to the Reserve Company for Rations and accommodation.

10. CODE WORD. The completion of Relief will be reported by Code Word "Wiring Finished".

11. A C K N O W L E D G E.

ISSUED AT.

Captain and Adjutant.

DISTRIBUTION.

Copy No				
1.	Commanding Officer.	No	2.	2nd in Command.
3.	Adjutant.		4.	"A" Company.
5.	"B" Company.		6.	"C" Company.
7.	"D" Company.		8.	H.Q. Company.
9.	Transport Officer.		10.	Quartermaster.
11.	Medical Officer.		12.	R.S.M.
13.	2/6th. Sher: Fors.		14.	178th Inf. Bde.
15.	10/11 H.L.Infantry.		16.	18th Welsh Regt.
17 & 18.	War Diary.		19.	File.

SECRET. OPERATION ORDERS No65 Copy No. 13

by

Major. C. [illegible]. C. TRENCH.

Commanding

2/5th Battalion. Sherwood Foresters.

.... 22.2.18.

War Diary.

INSTRUCTIONS. No1.

....

1. RELIEF. Companies will Parade ready to move off at the following times.

"B" Company.	6 p.m.	"D" Company.	6.15 p.m.
"A" Company.	6.30 p.m.	"C" Company and Wiring Platoon.	6.45 p.m.
Battalion Headquarters and R.A.P.			7 p.m.

Companies will move in Column of Route with 30 yards interval between Platoons.
Lewis Gun Wagons in rear of respective Companies.
Company Commanders will guide their Companies to CRUX CIRCUS. Company Commanders will be responsible for having their Companies organised into posts and Garrisons before they move off.

2. GUIDES. Guides will be provided as under :-

<u>Front Line Companies.</u>
1 guide for each Post.
1 for each Support Platoon.
1 for Company Headquarters.

<u>Support Company.</u>
1 for Company.

<u>Reserve Company & Battn: Hqrs.</u>
Nil.
Battalion Signallers 1.

R.A.P. 1.

3. BILLETS. The Battalion Intelligence Officer will report to Adjutant of 2/6th Sher. Fors. at 3.30 p.m. to reconnoitre accommodation for Hdqr's Company. He will be responsible for meeting Hdqr's Company and guiding them to their Billets. He will receive special instructions before leaving.

4. COOKING ARRANGEMENTS. The Support, Reserve and Headquarter Companies will Cook in RAILWAY RESERVE.
The two Front Line Companies will have their food cooked under the Quartermaster's arrangements.
There will be 15 Hot Food Containers available.
These are allotted as follows :-

Front Line Companies - 5 each.
Support Company - 5.

Front Line Companies will use 1 Hot Food Container for drawing Soup nightly from the Soup Kitchen for the front line Posts. The remainder for Front Line Companies will be sent down to the Quartermasters Stores by the R.S.M. on the night of the Relief.

5. TRENCH STORES. The R.S.M. will report to the 2/6th Bn S.F. at 3 p.m. and will take over all Battn. Trench Stroes. The Battn. Gas N.C.O. will report at same time to take over Battn. Gas Stores. and 1 N.C.O. per Company for Company Stores. Receipts will be given and a complete list of all stores taken over will be rendered by Companies to the Battn. Orderly Room by 5 p.m. D.R.L.S. of the 25th inst.

6. COMPULSORY GARRISONS. Compulsory Garrisons as under will be found by Coys: as mentioned in case of attack :-

<u>Strength.</u>	<u>Positions.</u>	<u>Found by.</u>
1 L.G. Team	[illegible] at U.19.c.[illegible]	Coy. in Support.

Para. 6. (Contd).	Strength.	Positions.	Found by.
	1 Platoon.	No.15 Post RAILWAY RESERVE. U.25.b.3.2.	Reserve Coy:
	1 Platoon.	No.16 Post. U.25.a.7.6.	Wiring Platoon.

7. ACKNOWLEDGE.

G. Andrews
Captain & Adjutant.

Issued at 2-10pm
Distribution :-
As for O.O.63 with exception of 17?th Inf.Bde & 2/6th S.F.

SECRET OPERATION ORDERS No. 63 Copy No... 12

by

Major C.E.C. TENCH, Commanding,
2/5th. Battalion, THE SHERWOOD FORESTERS.

....

22.2.1918.

ADMINISTRATIVE INSTRUCTIONS NO. 2.

1. TRANSPORT — Limber wagons will be allotted as follows :-
Front Line Companies 1 limber each
Support and Reserve Coys. 2 limbers each.
Battalion Headquarters 3 limbers.
The Transport Officer will arrange that these limbers report in Camp by 4 p.m.

2. STORES, KITS ETC. — All blankets, rolled tightly in bundles of 10 etc., will be ready in Company Huts by 8.30 a.m. Instructions will be issued in regard to handing over to representative of Quartermaster. Surplus Officers' Kits and Men's kits (in haversacks) will be handed to representative of Q.M. by 9.30 a.m. The Mess Cart will leave MORY CAMP at 4.30 p.m. with all Mess goods.

3. PERSONNEL — The following will remain at Quartermaster's Stores, in addition to Q.M's Stores and Transport personnel :-
Officers replaced by "Pool" Officers
Drums. Coy. Q.M. Sergts.,
Orderly Room Sergeant
Cooks of "B" and "D" Companies, and any cooks surplus to three in "A" and "C" Companies.
These details will leave MORY CAMP for Quartermaster's Stores at 5 p.m. under 2/Lt Dickinson who will be in charge.

4. WATER — The Water Duty Corporal will be responsible for having 6 water carts daily at CRUX CIRCUS, as follows :-
2 at 9.0 a.m.
2 at 2.0 p.m.
2 at 5.0 p.m.
Water duty men and horses will billet as before. In addition one water cart will accompany Battalion Headquarters to CRUX CIRCUS, where it will be emptied under arrangements made by the R.S.M. The Water Cart returning to ST LEGER.

5. RATIONS — The Quartermaster will arrange to deliver rations for the 24th. instant at MORY CAMP at 9.30 a.m. "B" and "D" Coys. will arrange for cooking their rations under instructions from the acting P.R.I. Rations for Headquarters , "A" & "C" Companies will be taken up uncooked. C.Q.M. Sergts will be responsible for seeing that these rations are loaded on to the limbers.

6. NOTICE BOARDS — Companies will render a return by "Returns Parade" on 26th. instant, as to the Notice Boards they require in their Sectors. Companies will keep a rough plan to show where notice boards are required to be handed over on relief.

7. SOCKS — The arrangements in force for last tour will hold good for this tour.

8. SALVAGE — Companies will arrange to send down all salvage material daily to Battalion Headquarters. A list of such salvage will be made in duplicate. When the salvage is handed to the R.S.M., he will sign one list as a receipt and file the other list. The R.S.M. will be responsible for seeing that all salvage on his dump is sent down to the Quartermaster daily, by the Sock wagon. He will obtain receipts for the same from the Quartermaster.

9. RETURNS: A Returns Parade will be held daily by the R.S.M. at 4 p.m. One Sergeant per Company will attend with all Routine Returns plus any special Returns asked for by the Battn: Orderly Room. The services of the Battn. D.R.L.S. will be utilised as far as possible by Companies for other "G" Returns.
D.Rs. will leave Battn : H.qrs daily for all Coys as under :-

5 a.m. 11 a.m. 5 p.m. 11 p.m.

H. Andrew
Captain & Adjutant.

Issued at 10.45 p.m.
Distribution :-
As for Administrative Instruction No.1.
plus :-
Water Duty Corporal.

War Diary

11

ORDERS No.1.
-- by --
MAJOR G. R.C.Trench.
Commanding
2/6th Battn: SHERWOOD FORESTERS.

Owing to possibility of an attack by the enemy on the Brigade Front and in order that the Battalion may be ready to move forward at a momemt's notice the following orders are issued :-

1. The Transport Officer willarrange to have four limber wagons permanently at North Camp, MORY. The limberswill be allotted one to each of "A", "B", "C" & "D" Companies. These limbers will report to Company Commanders to-morrow morning at 9.30 a.m. and will be available for the carriage of Lewis Guns and ammunition for same.

2. The Transport Officer will arrange for horses as under to be at the Camp within twenty-five minutes of receipt of code word "HUN".

(i) 8 horses for limbers as mentioned in para 1.

(ii) 3 Officers' mounts.

3. In the event of orders from Brigade being received to move forward, the undermentioned Officers are detailed to proceed as under :-

Captain Clifford ... Brigade Headquarters.
2/Lt. G R.MacDonald)
2/Lt. H.F.Barker) Battn: H.Qs of front Line Battalion.

4. ACKNOWLEDGE.

J.E.Andrews.
Captain & Adjutant.

Issued at 11-30 p.m.
Distribution :-
No.1. Commanding Officer.
2. 2nd in Command.
3. Adjutant.
4. "A" Company.
5. "B" Company.
6. "C" Company.
7. "D" Company.
8. "H.Q" Company.
9. Quartermaster.
10. Transport Officer.
11 & 12 War Diary.
13. File.

59th Division.

178th Infantry Brigade.

WAR
DIARY

2/5th BATTALION

THE SHERWOOD FORESTERS

MARCH 1 9 1 8

Instructions regarding War Diaries and Intelligence Summaries are contained in F. S. Regs., Part II. and the Staff Manual respectively. Title Pages will be prepared in manuscript.

WAR DIARY
or
~~INTELLIGENCE SUMMARY~~
(Erase heading not required.)

Army Form C. 2118.

178/592 2/5 Notts & Derby

Vol 14

2/5th BATTN. NOTTS & DERBY REGT.

Place	Date	Hour	Summary of Events and Information	Remarks and references to Appendices
	MARCH			
S. of CROISILLES	2		Battalion relieved in left subsector by 25th Northumberland Fusiliers and proceeded to MORY SOUTH Camp, 2/3.	See App "A" MWB
MORY	to		At MORY SOUTH; Training in progress & test standing to. All-night working parties every 3rd night at NOREUIL Camp improvements	MWB
NOREUIL	10		Battalion relieved 2/6th North Staffords in right sub-sector of right Brigade Front. B Company – Right Front, A " Centre ", & D C " Left " Support. Battalion H.Q., sunken road, C, 11, C, 65, 90. (57C NW)	" " "B" MWB
"	17		Battalion relieved by 7th Sherwood Foresters, & proceeded to Brigade Support. Battalion H.Q., ECOUST – NOREUIL Road.	MWB
"	21		Morning: Four hours bombardment followed by attack in force by the enemy (mass formation) who took 8 hours to penetrate 2000 yards. The battalion was eventually surrounded & cut off. Full report of this action is attached.	" " "C" MWB

2449 Wt. W14957/M90 750,000 1/16 J.B.C. & A. Forms/C.2118/12.

Instructions regarding War Diaries and Intelligence Summaries are contained in F. S. Regs., Part II. and the Staff Manual respectively. Title pages will be prepared in manuscript.

WAR DIARY

or

~~INTELLIGENCE SUMMARY.~~

(Erase heading not required.)

Army Form C. 2118.

Place	Date	Hour	Summary of Events and Information	Remarks and references to Appendices
ERVILLERS	21		Afternoon: Transport moved to COURCELLES, thence to camp at F17 d 22	MOB
	22		33 OR's under Captain QUIBELL sent up to right of MORY & remained there in opposition to counter-attacks -	MOB
SENLIS	23		Transport to SENLIS Draft of 23 O.R. arrived	MOB
	24		Reinforcements & survivors rejoin.	MOB
	25		Transport to BAVELINCOURT.	MOB MOB
BAVELIN-COURT	26		Transport to FIEFFES.	
FIEFFES	28		Transport by train to CAMBLIGNEUL.	MOB
CAMBLIGNEUL	30		Morning:- Visit to Battalion of His Majesty, KING GEORGE V. Afternoon:- Inspection by G.O.C., 59th Division.	MOB
			Effective Strength of Battn on 1/3/1918 = 48 Officers 950 Other Ranks Ration Strength of Battn on 31/3/1918 = 6 Officers 204 - Other Ranks	MOB

R. S. Pratt.
Major
Comdg 2/5th Bn Sherwood Foresters

D. D. & L., London, E.C. (A8001) Wt. W1771/M2031 750,000 5/17 Sch. 52 Forms C2118/14

"C"

2/5th Batt. SHERWOOD FORESTERS.

Report on operations for night 20/21st March onwards.

Reference Map. 57 C. N.W. 2. 1 /10,000.

In writing the account of the above action, difficulty is at once encountered, owing to the fact that all recordsincluding War Diary, Defence schemes, and Operation Orders were lost. Indeed the only information available is that afforded by messages sent to the Brigade H.Qs. during the action, and the statements of the four men who were the only suvivors.

On the night of March 20/21st, the 59th Division was holding the front line of the right flank of the 6th Corps round BULLECOURT. The 178th Inf. Bde. was holding the right forward sector, with the 7th Sherwoods on the right front, 2 /6th Sherwoods on the left front, and 2/5th Sherwoods in support immediately N. of the villiage of NOREUIL, the latter under the command of Lieut. Col. H.R. Gadd. M.C., with Major R.C. Trench as second in command.

DISPOSITIONS.

Battalion H.Qs. in the sunken road running from NOREUIL to LONGATTE about C.9.d.8.5. The remainder of the battalion in the trenches and sunken road round about IGAREE Corner at C.10.C.6.9.

An attack by the enemy in force had been expected for some days past.

At about 4.30 a.m. on the morning of March 21st, the enemy commenced a heavy bombardment on the whole area with Gas Shells. Gas Masks were immediately put on, and the Companies moved out to their stand-to positions :-

RIGHT FRONT:-	"B" Coy.	to NOREUIL SWITCH round C.5. C.4.4.
LEFT FRONT:-	"A" Coy.	to SYDNEY AVENUE round C.4.d.8.0.
SUPPORT COY:-	"D" Coy	to DEWSBURY TRENCH round C.10.B.7.4.
RESERVE COY:-	"C" Coy	to Sunken Road round C.9.d.8.5.

NARRATIVE.

At 5 a.m. the enemy commenced a heavy bombardment with H.E.

The following messages were received at Bde. H.Qs. :-

(~~2/Lieut. Williamson 7th Sherwood Foresters, Liason Officer~~)

Message by runner from 2/5th Sherwoods sent off at 7.5 a.m. " In communication with both front battalions, who report shelling general, but not very heavy AAA All battalions are being gassed AAA Greater part of shelling goingwest of NOREUIL -LONGATTE Road AAA No sigh of hostile attack as yet AAA"

Message by runner timed 8.30 a.m. " Hostile shelling still heavy , but gassing has ceased AAA Casualties do not appear to be heavy, but this is uncertain AAA"

2/Lieut Williamson , Liason Officer with Bde. H.Qs. went forward and sent back the following message by runner, timed 9.45 a.m. " Heavy Shelling of front line 2nd System, apparently from QUEANT and HENDECOURT AAA NOREUIL Valley heavily shelled AAA No aeroplane activity, and no machine gun

(Sheet No 2.)

gun fire . So far as can be ascertained the enemy barrage has not yet lifted from the front line
Message from 5th Sherwoods timed 10.4 0 a.m., by runner states " Enemy reported to be about C.11.a.1.5 Enemy barrage on PONTEFRACT, and DEWSBURY TRENCHES, and enemy advancing AAA Enemy also attacking near junction of ILKNEY SUPPORT, and HALIFAX AA
Further unconfirmed reports state :- Enemy have penetrated DEWSBURY AAA Am manning NOREUIL - LONGATTE Road , and ready to form defensive flanks to the right"
Message by runner from 2/5th Sherwoods timed 12 noon :- "Situation as follows :- We are holding NOREUIL SWITCH from C.9.d.9.4. and road near Batt. H.Qs. AAA Enemy have captured DEWSBURY and PONTEFRACT, and appear to be digging in AAA Have formed defensive flank down NOREUIL SWITCH from C.9.d.9.4. westwards. Enemy moving in large numbers along ridge C.17.C. AAA Am prolonging my line along road towards LONGATTE AAA Forces at my disposal estimated at 150. AAA

2/Lieut Williamson &th S.F. returned to Bde HQs. at 1 p.m. reported :- " At 10.15 when nearing the Battalion H.Qs. enemy creeping barrage lifted on to the NOREUIL- LONGATTE Road " He remained at H.Qs. until 12 noon, and then returned by NOREUIL Village and Valley, at which time the enemy were already in the villiage .

GENERAL.

The bombardment was apparently extremely heavy, commencing with gas shells and followed from 5 a.m. onwards with H.E.

The thickness of the fog made it extremely difficult for the men to see if the enemy were advancing, or whether our men were approaching.

The enemy appears to have pushed down the NOREUIL Valley in large numbers, and turning, to have attacked the Battalion on its flank.

From information gathered it is certain that the Battalion fought most gallantly, and the last message from Lieut/Col. Gadd bears this out.

CASUALTIES.

KILLED. Officers. 3

Major C.R.C. Trench.
2/Lt. F. Walters
" C.R. Brandeth.

Other Ranks. 3.

MISSING BELIEVED KILLED. Officers 1

Capt. R.J. Case.

Other Ranks x2.

WOUNDED & MISSING

Officers. 3

A/Capt. H. Waterhouse.
Lieut. R.E.E. Groner.
2/Lieut. P.A. Murphy.

Other Ranks 8.

(Sheet No 3)

MISSING. Officers. ~~24.~~ 22

Lt/Col. H.R. Gadd. M.C.
Lt. P.S. Whiston.
Lt. F.H. Sutherland
Lt. C.L. Wilkinson.
2/Lt. A.H. Chambers.
2/Lt. W. Hague.
2/Lt. R. Stone.
2/Lt. H.E. Barker.
2/Lt. L.J. de Mauny.
2/Lt. S.E. Grayson.
2/Lt. G.A. Middlemiss.
2/Lt. H.C. Pickhall.
2/Lt. W.S. Allen.
2/Lt. A.O. Robinson.
2/Lt. C.M. Wright.
2/Lt. W.W. Hacking.
2/Lt. A.E. Silverwood.
2/Lt. F.E. Andrews.
2/Lt. A.J. Smith.
2/Lt. T.W. Jago.
Capt. Mearns (R.A.M.C).
Capt. A.C. Judd (Chaplin attd.)

Other Ranks. 599.

WOUNDED. Officers 2.

Capt. T. Nadin. (Bde. H.Q. Staff)
Capt. W.N. Wright do

Other Ranks 12.

SUVIVORS. Other Ranks 4.

SECRET.

War Diary

OPERATION ORDER No.64.
by
Major C.R.Chenevix Trench
Commanding,
2/5th Bn. The Sherwood Foresters.

Copy No. 12 "A"

1.3.1918.

1.INTENTION. The Battalion will be relieved in the Left sub-sectoron the night of the 2/3rdinstant by the 25th Battn.Northumberland Fusiliers and will proceed to MORY South Camp where it will be in Divisional Reserve.

2.TIMES & ORDER OF RELIEF. The relief will take place after dark.
All Companies in this Sector will be relieved by corresponding Companies of the relieving Battalion.

3.GUIDES. Guides as under will be provided :-
(a) 1 for Battn. Headquarters.
1 per Company
1 for R.A.P.
to be at 178th Infantry Brigade Headquarters (L'HOMME MORT) at 6.45 p.m. The guides as above will parade outside Battn. Orderly Room at 5.15 p.m. under L/C Barrowclough.

(b) 1 guide per post and one for remainder of Coy: for Front Line Companies.
1 guide per Platoon for Support Company.
1 Guide for Reserve Company.
The guides as in sub-para (b) to parade outside Battn Orderly Room at 6.0 p.m. under 2/Lt. G.Manning.
Each guide will be in possession of a piece of paper shewing the number of post, number of platoon and designation of Company for which he is acting as gùide.
In addition each Front Line Company will send an Officer to superintend the organisation of the guides for the front ɲ line posts etc.

4.HANDING OVER. (1) All Defence Scemes. Maps, photos, trench and area stores will be handed over on relief and receipts taken. All receipts to be sent to Battn. Headquarters by "Returns Parade" on the 3rd instant.
(2) All Trenches in the sector and all accommodation will be handed over cleanand tidy and a Certificate to this effect will be obtained from the relieving Battalion by Company Commanders.

5.PATROLS. Each Front Line Company will send out a Covering Patrol during the time the relief is in pr ogress which will be withdrawn by the Company Commander when the relief is complete.

6.COMPLETION OF RELIEF. Company Commanders will report personally at Battn. Headquarters as they leave the area that their Company relief is complete.

7. ACKNOWLEDGE.

Issued at 12 midnight

Captain & Adjutant.

Distribution :-
1. Commanding Officer.
2. 2nd in Command.
3. Adjutant.
4. "A" Coy.
5. "B" Coy.
6. "C" Coy.
7. "D" Coy.
8. "H.Q" Coy.
9. 25th N.F.
10. 178th Inf Bde.
11. Q.M. & Transport.
12 & 13. War Diary.
14. File.

SECRET. *War Diary*

"A" 12

OPERATION ORDER No. 64   Copy No. *12*

by

Major C.F. Chenevix Trench

Commanding.

2/5th Bn. The Sherwood Foresters.   1.3.18.

ADMINISTRATIVE ---------- INSTRUCTION No1.

1. BILLETTING PARTY. A Billetting Party as under will report to 2/Lt. H.D. Barrows at 11 a.m. outside Battn: Orderly Room:-
   Each Company ... 1 N.C.O. & 4 men
   Battn Hdqrs. ... 1 N.C.O. & 2 men.
   This party will proceed to MORY South Camp and allot accommodation.

2. GUIDES. 2/Lt. H.D. Barrows will arrange to have guides as under :-
   4 for each Company.
   2 for Battn. Hdqrs.
   to be at Haystack by L'HOMME MORT at 9.30 p.m.
   These guides will conduct Companies to their new quarters.

3. COMPANY STORES. Companies will arrange to dump their Lewis Guns and ammunition, also Company Stores at CRUX CIRCUS as they pass after relief from the line. A loading party of 1 N.C.O. and 2 men per Company will be detailed to remain with limbers to load these stores. Companies will arrange with the R.S.M. as to the exact position of their Dump beforehand. A.P. & Tracer S.A.A. will NOT be handed over but brought down and dumped at Company Dump at CRUX CIRCUS.

4. COOKING UTENSILS. The Sergeant Cook will arrange for the collection and dumping of all cooking utensils at CRUX CIRCUS by 7.30 p.m. Company Commanders will each detail one cook to assist the Sergeant Cook and the remaining cooks will march with their Companies.

5. WATER CANS. All Water cans will be delivered to the R.S.M. by 3.30p.m. It is of the utmost importance that the strictest attention is paid to this.

6. TRANSPORT. The Transport Officer will arrange for limbers as follows:-

Rendezvous.	Time.	No of Limbers	Purpose.
CRUX CIRCUS.	7.30 p.m.	2.	*Cooking Utensils.* H.Q.Mess.
-- do --	9.30p.m.	5.	Lewis Guns Coy Stores Battn Stores.

7. SUPPER. The Quartermaster will arrange for Hot Tea to be available for Companies on reaching Camp.

8. OFFICERS' KITS. The Quartermaster will arrange for all Company Mess Stores and Officers' Kits to be available at MORY South Camp to-morrow. These Kits will be distributed to respective Officers' Messes & huts under directions from 2/Lt. H.D. Barrows.
   The Quartermaster will arrange for all blankets to be taken up Camp and distributed to C.Q.M.Ss. to-morrow morning.

9. WATERCARTS. The Transport Officer will arrange for Watercarts and personnel to leave ST LEGER at 4 p.m. to-morrow and to report at MORY Camp South.

Issued at *12 midnight.*   Captain & Adjutant.

Distribution :-
As for Operation Order No.64
less :-
178th Inf Bde.
25th N.F.

War Diary

"A"
13

ORDERS
- by -
MAJOR C.R. Chenevix Trench.
Commanding,
2/5th Bn. The Sherwood Foresters.

5.3.1918.

Provisional Order re "Standing to" issued to-day is cancelled and the following substituted.

A real or practice "Stand to" may occur at any time.
On receipt of message "Stand to", all ranks will turn out in Full Marching Order, less Greatcoats.
The Battalion will parade in mass on ground facing the Orderly Room.
Order of Coys: from right to left :- H.Qs."A" "B" "C" "D".

The following will be specially noted :-

(1) All other ranks will have their full Marching Order together at all times unless otherwise ordered.

(2) Lewis Gun limbers will be loaded ready to move off at any time. Guns in use by the class being replaced in the wagons immediately the Class is finished each day.

(3) Greatcoats will be left in each man's place on the floor of the hut.
Hairy coats or Jerkins will be worn.

(4) The same personnel as were left out of the line last time will remain in Camp until they get orders.

(5) All Waterbottles will be kept full.

(6) The Sergeant Cook will arrange for the Kitchens to be loaded immediately.

(7) Watercarts will be held in readiness to move.

(8) The Transport Officer will immediately despatch horses for the Kitchens and Watercarts and report at the Orderly Room in Camp.

E. Andrews.
Captain & Adjutant

Issued at 7.15 p.m.
Distribution :-
1. Commanding Officer.
2. 2nd in Command.
3. Adjutant & File.
4. "A" Coy:
5. "B" Coy:
6. "C" Coy:
7. "D" Coy:
8. H.Qs. "
9. Transport Officer.
10. Quartermaster.
11. R.S.M.
12. Sergeant Cook.
13 & 14. War Diary.

SECRET   Copy No. 14 "B"

War Diary

OPERATION ORDERS No. 65
by
Lieut. Colonel H.R. GADD M.C.,
Commanding,
2/5th. Battalion, The Sherwood Foresters.

9.3.1918.

REFERENCE MAP CHERISY 1/10,000 and 57 c N.W. 1/20,000.

1. INTENTION. The Battalion will relieve the 2/6th. South Staffords, in the Right Sub-sector of the Right Brigade Front on the evening of the 10th. instant.

2. DISPOSITION. Companies will relieve as under :-

Sector.	2/5th. Sherwoods	2/6th. S.Staffs.
Right	"B" Coy.	"A" Coy.
Centre	"A" Coy.	"C" Coy.
Left	"C" Coy.	"D" Coy.
Support	"D" Coy.	"B" Coy.

Battalion Headquarters will be in sunken road, near junction of DEWSBURY TRENCH and HOBART AVENUE.
R.A.P. will be at Battalion Headquarters.

3. GUIDES Guides will meet the Battalion at a time to be notified later at SUGAR FACTORY (B.24.d.75.75.)
They will wear a white arm band, and each have a paper containing written instructions.
Companies will relieve in the order, Headquarters, Left Front, Centre Front, Right Front and Support.

4. PATROLS Patrolling for the night 10/11th. will be carried out by the 2/6th. S. Staffs., but each Company in the Front Line will send one N.C.O. and 2 men with each patrol to pick up information and landmarks. These will report at Battalion Headquarters of 2/6th. S. Staffs., at 3 p.m. on the 10th. inst.

5. WIRING. The Wiring Platoon, composed as detailed by the Adjutant, will be formed under the command of Sergt. WILLIAMS. This Platoon will be accommodated and rationed by the Support Company.

6 COOKING Cooking will be done as under :-
Centre, Left and Support Companies in RAILWAY RESERVE.
Right Company near Right Company Headquarters . Battalion Headquarters at Battalion Headquarters.

7. RATIONS AND WATER Rations will be brought up by limber wagons as far as Battalion Headquarters, and each Company willsend a carrying party for them from this point.
Water may be obtained in the following way :-
(a) From Water Carts at Battalion Headquarters, which can only be refilled at night.
(b) By carriage from NOREUIL.
(c) From Water Tanks in Left Sector, which are not yet complete.

8. SOCKS. The usual procedure for supplying dry socks will be employed. For 1st. day the situation will be :-
one pair on man, one pair in pack (reserve) and one pair at Company Headquarters.
Each night dirty socks will be send down to Battalion Headquarters and the same number of new pairs taken over in exchange.

9. R.E. DUMP The R.E. Dump is situated at IGAREE CORNER, C.10.c.65.90.

10. DRESS Dress will be marching order less Haversaks. All personal property will be put into haversacks, which will be returned to Q.M's. Stores.

11. DEFENCE SCHEMES, MAPS ETC.
All Maps, Defence Schemes, Trench and Area Stores, will be taken over and receipts given. All lists of Stores will be handed in to Orderly Room by 12 noon 11th. instant.

12. COMPLETION OF RELIEF.

Company Commanders will report completion of relief of their Company by Code Word "SELDA".

13. ACKNOWLEDGE.

[signature]

Captain and Adjutant,
2/5th. Battalion, The Sherwood Foresters.

ISSUED AT 6.15 p.m.

DISTRIBUTION.

Copy No.
1 Commanding Officer
2. 2nd. in Command
3 Adjutant
4 O.C. "A" Coy.
5 O.C. "B" Coy.
6 O.C. "C" Coy.
7 O.C. "D" Coy.
8 O.C. H.Q. Coy.
9 Transport Officer.
10 Quartermaster
11 R.S.M.
12 178th. Infantry Brigade.
13 2/6th. S. Staffs.
14 & 15 War Diary
16 File.

SECRET.

"B" 1A

OPERATION ORDERS No. 65
- by -
Lieut-Colonel H.R.Gadd. M.C.
Commanding,
2/5th Bn. THE SHERWOOD FORESTERS. 9.3.1918.

ADMINISTRATIVE INSTRUCTIONS, No. 1.

Ref. Map CHERISY 1/10,000 and 57.c.N.W. 1/20,000.

1. CORRECTIONS. Ref. Operation Orders No.65, para 1. for "2/6th South Staffords" read "2/6th North Staffords".
Ref. para 7, erase that portion dealing with "rations"
" " 8, erase last two lines.

2. RATIONS. Rations for four Companies will come up by Railway as far as NOREUIL, where they will be met by Battn: Pushing Party which will push them to the point whence they are fetched by Company Ration Parties.
H.Q.Coy and Battn: Hdqrs Rations will be brought up by limbers nightly to Battn. Hdqrs.

3. SOCKS. L/Cpl: Lewendon will be in charge of socks at Battn: Hdqrs: All dirty socks will be returned to him by 3 p.m. daily, and a similar number of new ones drawn in exchange.

4. WORK. The Support Company will find the following permanent Working Parties :-

8 a.m. - 2 p.m.	6 O.R. at Bn. Hdqrs.
2 p.m. - 8 p.m.	12 - do - do
8 p.m. - 2 a.m.	1 N.C.O. & 10 men at R.E.Dump IGAREE CORNER.

The 8.0 p.m. party will be taken over by Support Coy: to-morrow night. They will go up with Battn.Hdqrs; party, leave their packs at Battn. Hdqrs and go back to IGAREE CORNER.

5. DRUMS. The Drums will find the following parties :-
1 N.C.O. & 3 men - L.G.Guard, Q.M.Stores.
3 Drummers. - L.G.Guard: Battn.Hdqrs.
Orders for remainder will be issued later.

6. KITS, WAGONS, etc.
(a) All blankets and haversacks will be stacked where L.G.Limber Horses now are at 9.0 a.m. The Orderly Officer will superintend.
(b) Officers' store Kits will be stacked at the same place at 2.30 p.m.
(c) The Mess Cart will be loaded with Stores, Mess Kit at same place at 4.30 p.m.
(d) Field Kitchens will be removed by 5.0 p.m. Teas will be at 4.0 p.m.
(e) Limbered Wagons - 1 per Coy for L.G.Guns, Officers' Trench Kits etc, and one for Cooking utensils of "A" & "B" Coys and 1 for "C" & "D" Coys, and 3 for H.Qs. will be at Battn: Hdqrs at 4.0 p.m.
The A/R.S.M. will superintend the allotment and loading of these limbors.

7. ORDER OF MARCH. Companies will move from present Camp as under :-

Hdqrs	-	6.15 p.m.
"C" Coy:	-	6.20 p.m.
"A" "	-	6.30 p.m.
"B" "	-	6.40 p.m.
"D" "	-	6.50 p.m.

All movement after passing Sugar Factory, B.24.d.8.8. will be by Platoons at 200 yards interval.

8. INSPECTION. The Commanding Officer will inspect the Camp at 4.0 p.m. when Companies will arrange to have their areas ready for inspection.

9. ACKNOWLEDGE.

[signature]

Captain & Adj.

Issued at 2.0 a.m. (10.3.18)

DISTRIBUTION :-

1. Commanding Officer.
2. 2nd.in Command.
3. Adjutant.
4. "A" Coy:
5. "B" "
6. "C" "
7. "D" "
8. "H.Q" "
9. Transport Officer.
10. Quartermaster.
11. R.S.M.
12. 2/6th N.Staffs.
13.)
14.) War Diary.
15. File.

SECRET. 2/5th. Battalion, The Sherwood Foresters. Copy No. 13

DEFENCE SCHEME

W.D. [handwritten]

LEFT SUB SECTOR

In continuation of and supercession of Operation Order No. 66 para. 4, and Instructions No. 1, para. 6.

1. DISPOSITION.

The Front Line consists of a series of Posts, numbered Nos. 1 - 11, running out of TUNNEL TRENCH. Of these posts No. 9 is only manned at night.
The Support Line is BURG SUPPORT, and the Reserve Line will be TIGER TRENCH, and STRAY RESERVE in U 13 d.
At present TIGER TRENCH is not completed.
The Support Company is situated in STRAY RESERVE and the Reserve Company at T 24.d.
Battalion Headquarters is located in RAILWAY RESERVE near CRUX CIRCUS.

2. BOUNDARIES.

Right Battalion Boundary. U 15 d central - VULCAN STRONG POINT exclusive - JOVE LANE - QUEEN'S LANE - STRAY RESERVE inclusive - U 19 d 9.6. - U 26.a.00.40 - U 25.b.8.1.
Left Battalion Boundary. U 14 a.70.13 - U 14.c.28.80 (HUMP LANE exclusive) - U 13.d.9.8. - T 24.b.5.2. - T 30.a 2.7. - T 29.a.00.90 - T 22.d.5.2. - T 28.a.00.40
The dividing line between Companies will be KNUCKLE AVENUE.

3. ACTION IN CASE OF ATTACK.

In case of attack the Battalion may be considered under two headings :-
(a) Garrisons of certain lines and localities which must be held at all costs no matter what the situation is, or to what depth the enemy has penetrated.
(b) Counter-attack formations.

4. GARRISONS

Locality	Garrison	Strength
Line of Posts and BURY SUPPORT	Right and Left Front Companies	2 Companies.
STRAY RESERVE about U 19.d.9.9.	1 Lewis Gun and Team	Support Coy,
No. 15 Post RAILWAY RESERVE U 25.b.8.2.	Wiring Platoon	1 Officer, 28 Other Ranks
No. 16 Post, RAILWAY RESERVE U 25 a.90.60	Reserve Coy.	1 Platoon

5. COUNTER ATTACK FORMATION.

In case of attack the Support Company will man STRAY RESERVE from MAN RESERVE to Left Battalion Boundary. This Company will be available for counter- attack at the discretion of Officer Commanding Company, but counter-attack should not be made if possible until reinforcements have been received from the Rear to man this defensive line.
The Reserve Company will " Stand To" in the following positions
1 Platoon U 25 a.55.70
1 Platoon U 19.c.25.25
1 Platoon T 24.d.70.15
These three Platoons of this Company will not be used for counter- attack until their places are taken by Platoons from th Reserve Battalion.

6. DEFENSIVE FLANKS

All Communication Trenches will be used if the necessity arises as Defensive Flanks. In this connection as there is no continuous Communication Trench on the left of the Battalion, that flank will be protected by fire from STRAY RESERVE , between U.19.b.85.50 and U 13.d.60.20.

7. GENERAL INSTRUCTIONS.

If Tanks are used by the enemy, they should be allowed to pass. Riflemen will direct their fire on the Infantry following the Tanks, and Lewis Guns will use their special ammunition against the Tanks at short ranges. Arrangements also have been made by ~~with~~ the Artillery for dealing with Tanks should they be employed.

8. ANTI-AIR CRAFT DEFENCES

Lewis Guns will be mounted as under :-

LOCALITY	BY WHOM FOUND
Battalion Headquarters.	Reserve Company.
BURY SUPPORT	Support Company.

9. WORKING PARTIES.

(a) In case of attack working parties on the Front Line System will occupy the nearest trenches and at once report to the nearest Company Headquarters.

(b) Any working parties of the Reserve Company that are detailed for permanent garrisons and the Wiring Platoon will at once proceed to their Posts.

(c) The remainder of the working parties of the Reserve Company will report to the nearest Company Headquarters where they will receive instructions sent by the Commanding Officer.

10. ACKNOWLEDGE.

Captain and Adjutant.
2/5th. Battalion, The Sherwood Foresters.

DISTRIBUTION.

Copy No.	
1	Commanding Officer
2	2nd. in Command
3	Adjutant
4	O.C. "A" Coy.
5	O.C. "B" Coy.
6	O.C. "C" Coy.
7	O.C. "D" Coy.
8	O.C. Headquarters
9	178th. Infantry Brigade.
10	O.C. Right Front Battalion
11	O.C. Relieving Battalion.
12	File
13 & 14	War Diary.

SECRET.

War Diary

Copy No. 15.....

TRENCH SCHEME.
Infantry Section.

2/5th Battn. THE SHERWOOD FORESTERS
holding RIGHT FRONT SECTOR.
(Cancelling Orders No. 65).

14.5.18.

Ref. Map HENDECOURT Special Sheet 1/20,000.

1. DISPOSITIONS. Three Companies hold the Front Line System, and one Company with one Company of Support Battalion, holds the Reserve Line, and are available for a Battalion Counter attack.

(a) Right Front Company holds HALIFAX Support from its junction with HOBART to the Railway (exclusive) with three platoons, and is covered by the fourth platoon holding a line of posts in the Front Line.

(b) Centre Front Company holds ILKLEY Support from the Railway (inclusive) and GOOLE Alley as far as HORSESHOE Support with three platoons and is covered by the fourth Platoon holding a line of posts in the front Line.

(N.B.) The positions and number of the Front Line posts in (a) and (b) is immaterial, and they may be constantly changed as long as they command the lines of approach.

(c) Left Front Company holds HORSESHOE Support from GOOLE to C.5.a.7.7. where it joins the Left Battn: with two platoons, and is covered by the other two Platoons holding a line of posts along ROTHERHAM Alley and RACK Trench (YORK Trench).

The positions and Garrisons of these Posts are as under :-

Junction of ROTHERHAM and Front Line - 1 Section
SHEFFIELD Sap, U.29.d.6.2. - 1 Lewis Gun Section
1 Rifle Bombing Sec
and Four Section Posts in RACK Trench.

(d) The Support Company is accommodated in RAILWAY Reserve near its junction with ILKLEY and HALIFAX, and is responsible for the defence of NEW Trench from SYDNEY Cross to C.11.a.3.9. from which point the Company of the Support Battalion from IGAREE Corner is responsible as far as DEWESBURY.

2. ACTION IN CASE OF ATTACK.

(a) In case of attack all men in front, Support, or reserve Line will hold their ground even if the enemy has penetrated on their flanks.

(b) If any portion of the Front or Support Line is penetrated the Company Commanders will immediately counter attack with all troops they can spare taking into consideration the importance of defending their own ~~portion of~~ the Support Line.

(c) If the Battalion Commander considers he can best check the enemy's advance by counter attacking he may do so with either one or both of the Companies in NEW Trench. Sufficient troops must, however, always be left in NEW Trench for its defence. The Counter attack might take the form of an attack against advancing Infantry or a more deliberate attack against some portion of our linepenetrated by the enemy. In either case it would be unlikely that Artillery co-operation will be available. The most likely cases will be as under :-
Right Company - Attack against HOBART Avenue. In which case the attackers would dribble man by man into SUNKEN Road C.11.a.6.2. where they will form up and attack in conjunction with a party working along SUNKEN Road C.11.central.
Attack against HALIFAX.
In which case a Frontal attack would be made.
Left Company -
Attack against the Railway in C.5.d.
This would be made by a Frontal attack assisted by attack Eastwards along the Railway.
Attack against Trench Junctions :
GOOLE, SYDNEY, HORSESHOE, SHEFFIELD; In which case the attack would form up on the Railway.

3. LOCATIONS. Battalion Headquarters. Sunken Road at Junction of HOBART and DEWSBURY.

Right Front Company.	C.11.b.3.8.
Centre Front Company.	C.5.d.4.8.
Left Front Company.	C.5.b.75.65.
Support Company.	C.5.d.70.65.
R.A.P.	Battalion Headquarters.

4 Acknowledge

E. Andrews
Captain & Adjutant.
2/5th Bn. Sherwood Foresters.

Issued at ....
Distribution :-
Copy No.1. Commanding Officer.
2. 2nd in Command.
3. Adjutant.
4. O.C."A" Coy.
5. O.C."B" "
6. O.C."C" "
7. O.C."D" "
8. O.C."H.Q""
9. 178th Inf Bde.
10. Relieving Battn.
11. Right Battn:
12. Left Battn:
13. Medical Officer.
14. File.
15 & 16. War Diary.

Orders No 69.
by
Lieut Colonel. H.R. Gadd. M.C.
Commanding.
2/5th Battalion. Sherwood Foresters. 19/3/18.

1. The following will reconnoitre the Left Subsector of the Right Brigade Front tomorrow 20th inst.
   2nd in Command
   4 Company Commanders.
   Intelligence Officer.
   The above Officers will report at Headquarters 2/6th Battalion. Sherwood Foresters at 10.30 am.
2. Subsectors will be taken over as under:—
   Right Front. "C" Company
   Left —"— "B" —"—
   Right Reserve "A" —"—
   Left —"— "D" —"—
3. If visibility is bad the party will proceed in pairs along Dead Mule Valley in C4C to the Headquarters Left Front Battalion.
4. The Commanding Officer thinks that the present Front Line is held too strongly and the Support Line too weakly. Reconnaissance should determine the views of the Company Commanders concerned on this subject.
5. Arrangements will be made to take over the line from 2/6th exactly as they are holding it at present.
6. Acknowledge.

[signature]
Captain & Adjutant.

Copy No. 10.

Orders No 15
by
Lieut. Colonel N.C. Rado M.C.
Commanding
5th Battalion Sherwood Foresters

Reference Map. Sheet 57B. S.W.

1. Distribution.

(a) The Right Front Company will hold KAVVAK SUPPORT between HOBART and RAILWAY RESERVE with 3 Platoons. The 4th Platoon will find 3 posts in the Front Line covering them.

(b) The Centre Front Company will hold ILKLEY SUPPORT between RAILWAY RESERVE and U29 d 8.1. with 3 Platoons the 4th Platoon finding 3 Posts in the Front Line covering them.

(c) The Left Front Company will hold YORK TRENCH between U29 a. [illegible] and its junction with [illegible] TRENCH with 3 Platoons covered by 1 Platoon finding 4 Posts as under:-

(1) Junction of Rotherham Alley and Front Line
(2) U29. d. 6.9.
(3) U29 d. 5.7.
(4) U29 d. 3.9.

(d) The Support Company will be accommodated in RAILWAY RESERVE about C5a. 6.7. but in case of attack or "Stand To" will man that portion of NOREUIL SWITCH between SIDNEY CROSS and C11 a. 3.9.

(e) The Company of the SUPPORT BATTN at FORKED CORNER will in case of attack man that portion of the [illegible] SWITCH between [illegible]

and DEWSBURY TRENCH.
They will come under the orders of O.C. Right Sector.

2. Action in Case of Attack

In case of attack all men of the Front Companies hold their ground, the Main Line being the Support Line.
Only if the Front Line is penetrated by very small numbers will a Counter Attack be made.
The Company in NOREUIL SWITCH between DEWSBURY TRENCH and SIDNEY CROSS will hold their ground at all costs but may be used for Counter Attack by order of Battalion Commander.

Acknowledge.
Issued at p.m.

J. E. Andrews
Captain & Adjutant
2/5th Battalion, Sher: Fors.

Distribution.

No. 1. Commanding Officer.
2. 2nd in Command.
3. Adjutant.
4. A. Coy.
5. B. Coy.
6. C. Coy.
7. D. Coy
8. 170th Infantry Brigade.
9. O.C. 2/6 Notts & Derby. Rgt.
10. " 2/7 -"- -"- -"-
11. East. Kent. Rgt.

Copy of letter from Br.-General.T.W.Stansfield. CMG.DSO.

64 Seabrook Road
HYTHE. Kent.

23.11.32.

Director,
Historical Section,

Herewith 3 letters

1. from Lt.-Col. Gadd
2. " Major A.C.Clarke
3. " Capt. Greaves.

also one from Gen. Haldane giving his views after reading Col. Gadd's letter.

Please make what use of them you like and return them to me when finished with.

(sgd) T.W.Stansfield.
Br.-Gen.

. . . .

Copy of letter from Lt.-Col. H. R. GADD (commdg. 2/5 Sherwood Foresters) to Br.-General T. W. Stansfield.

Hertford.

19th December 1918.

Dear General,

I returned from Germany early last week and very pleased was I to do so. I met Hodgson yesterday and he told me you were still commdg. the 178th I.B. and so I hasten to let you know what happened on March 21st. I am not quite certain of all the times etc. as my memory got very bad in Germany.

About 5 a.m. the German barrage and bombardment started and they filled the Sunken road with gas shells at the same time. There was little doubt that this was the preliminary of the big show, and I posted my Intelligence Officer where he could see most of our front telling him to look out for the S.O.S. As you know it was very misty and the S.O.S. was never seen, in fact there was no indication when the enemy attacked. Soon after 9 a.m. the enemy was first seen in masses moving on the ridge S. of Noreuil in the 6th Div. area. We took them on with 2 L.G's but they were a long way off. About the same time the Bde. signallers intercepted a message on the Power Buzzer from Hodgkin (Lt.-Col. commdg. 2/6 Sherwood Foresters) saying his front line had been penetrated. Between 10 and 11 a.m. my front Coys. became engaged, not by a large attack from the front but by the enemy working up the valleys on either side, especially the Noreuil side. They also came down Sydney Street. These coys. put up a good fight I think as I had messages from them during the fighting, but the end in each case was the same. They were attacked from the rear and front and bombed up from the flanks. I had no news from my coy. in Noreuil Switch, but judging from the shell fire I think they had little chance, and probably went the way of the 6th and 7th Battns. Meanwhile I had moved my Reserve Coy., sending some to garrison Noreuil Switch near the Sunken Road, and the others along the Sunken Road. We commanded the Noreuil Valley on the right and I had the valley on the left watched by patrols.

After about 11 o'clock everything became very quiet and we spent the time organizing the defence of the Sunken Road. There was a lot of sniping and now Trench was hit for the second time in the head, after which he soon died. In spite of everything I was feeling very optimistic, thinking we had stopped the advance. There was, however, a continual enemy movement in the 6th Div. area. The enemy could be seen digging in on the ridge near Toller's (Lt.-Col., commdg. 2/7th Sherwood Foresters) H.Q., which strengthened the idea that he had been stopped. Our left seemed pretty quiet.

About 1 p.m. I got your message saying that the Lincolns were occupying the trench about 400 yards to our rear, and the runner who brought the message said he had seen them there.

Shortly after this I became aware that the enemy had got Ecoust, although they had had it apparently for some time. I ought to have found this out sooner.

This news, and the fact that the movement on the right continued, made me decide to go back to the trench 400 yards to the rear, now occupied by the Lincolns. I ordered men to get back in small groups, and about 2 p.m. started back with Andrews, but ran slap into about 200 Bosche's coming straight up from the rear, and we were caught. I believe the Lincoln's had been mopped up about 2 hours before, anyhow I saw them as prisoners afterwards.

So ended the 21st March as far as the 2/5th was concerned. How much we did to stop the advance I don't know, but I think we succeeded in spreading our departure over a considerable time. I was sorry to lose Trench, he was doing very brave things at the time, organizing the defences etc.

There are a few more details I could give and I should like to see you when you are home.

Yours sincerely,

(sgd) H.R.Gadd.

(commdg. 2/5th Sherwood Foresters)

Copy of letter from Lt.-Col.H.R.GADD (commdg. 2/5 Sherwood Foresters) to Br.-General T.W.Stansfield.

Hertford.

19th December 1918.

Dear General,

I returned from Germany early last week and very pleased was I to do so. I met Hodgson yesterday and he told me you were still commdg. the 178th I.B. and so I hasten to let you know what happened on March 21st. I am not quite certain of all the times etc. as my memory got very bad in Germany.

About 5 a.m. the German barrage and bombardment started and they filled the Sunken road with gas shells at the same time. There was little doubt that this was the preliminary of the big show, and I posted my Intelligence Officer where he could see most of our front telling him to look out for the S.O.S. As you know it was very misty and the S.O.S. was never seen, in fact there was no indication when the enemy attacked. Soon after 9 a.m. the enemy was first seen in masses moving on the ridge S. of Noreuil in the 6th Div. area. We took them on with 2 L.G's but they were a long way off. About the same time the Bde. signallers intercepted a message on the Power Buzzer from Hodgkin (Lt.-Col. commdg. 2/6 Sherwood Foresters) saying his front line had been penetrated. Between 10 and 11 a.m. my front Coys. became engaged, not by a large attack from the front but by the enemy working up the valleys on either side, especially the Noreuil side. They also came down Sydney Street. These coys. put up a good fight I think as I had messages from them during the fighting, but the end in each case was the same. They were attacked from the rear and front and bombed up from the flanks. I had no news from my coy. in Noreuil Switch, but judging from the shell fire I think they had little chance, and probably went the way of the 6th and 7th Battns. Meanwhile I had moved my Reserve Coy., sending some to garrison Noreuil Switch near the Sunken Road, and the others along the Sunken Road. We commanded the Noreuil Valley on the right and I had the valley on the left watched by patrols.

After about 11 o'clock everything became very quiet and we spent the time organizing the defence of the Sunken Road. There was a lot of sniping and now French was hit for the second time in the head, after which he soon died. In spite of everything I was feeling very optimistic, thinking we had stopped the advance. There was, however, a continual enemy movement in the 6th Div. area. The enemy could be seen digging in on the ridge near Toller's (Lt.-Col., commdg. 2/7th Sherwood Foresters) H.Q., which strengthened the idea that he had been stopped. Our left seemed pretty quiet.

About 1 p.m. I got your message saying that the Lincolns were occupying the trench about 400 yards to our rear, and the runner who brought the message said he had seen them there.

Shortly, after this I became aware that the enemy had got Ecourt, although they had had it apparently for some time. I ought to have found this out sooner.

This news, and the fact that the movement on the right continued, made me decide to go back to the trench 400 yards to the rear, now occupied by the Lincolns. I ordered men to get back in small groups, and about 2 p.m. started back with Andrews, but ran slap into about 200 Bosche's coming straight up from the rear, and we were caught. I believe the Lincoln's had been mopped up about 2 hours before, anyhow I saw them as prisoners afterwards.

So ended the 21st March as far as the 2/5th was concerned. How much we did to stop the advance I don't know, but I think we succeeded in spreading our departure over a considerable time. I was sorry to lose Trench, he was doing very brave things at the time, organizing the defences etc.

There are a few more details I could give and I should like to see you when you are home.

Yours sincerely,

(sgd) H.R.Gadd.

(commdg. 2/5th Sherwood Foresters)

Copy of letter from Major A.C.Clarke. (2nd-in-Command, 2/6th Sherwood Foresters) to Br.-General T.W.Stansfield.)

January 14/19.

March 21st, 1918.

During the night 20/21st March, our artillery did a great deal of firing, but after 2 a.m. on 21st very few shells came over. Weather fine but misty.

5 a.m. Enemy bombardment opened - guns of all calibres being used against our Reserve trenches - Trench Mortars were chiefly used against our front and support lines. A large quantity of gas shells were used. All communications were destroyed as soon as the bombardment began. The shelling continued with great intensity until 9 a.m. From 7.15 to 9 a.m. hurricane bombardment. The front line was completely obliterated and considerable damage was done to the Reserve Line. "Battle positions" were manned soon after 5 a.m. As soon as it was light enough to see I went up to Post No.18 to find out what the situation was.

9 a.m. Enemy reported to be advancing. I at once went up to Post No.18 and saw the Bosche moving forward from his support line in 3 waves - 50 yards between each - a line of mopper's up followed the first wave. I then ran down to B.H.Q. dug-out to inform the C.O., and

9.20 a.m. on my way back to Post No.18, put up 2 S.O.S. rockets, one having been previously put up. The enemy on our immediate front moved slowly forward to the dead ground East of our front line - meanwhile I noticed large numbers of Bosche moving West, on the high ground - the spurs running East of Ecouste & Noreuil, north and south of us respectively. I at once ordered fire to be opened on them, they being some 800 - 1,000 yards away. There was no reply to our S.O.S. except a few heavies. Enemy barrage on Rly. Reserve still continued and men were continually hit. Owing to the formation of the two spurs mentioned, the enemy disappeared from view soon after fire was opened. I next saw the enemy moving forward from the dead ground in front of us and at once went down to inform the C.O., and returned (to) Post No.18 almost at the same time. Crowds of Bosche appeared on the high ground S. of us - 400 yards away, and these began to enfilade us with M.G's and rifle fire. We were also being enfiladed from the high ground North of us. I immediately ordered all available men to fire on the enemy South of us, as they were densely packed in large numbers (some 200 of them) at the same time I ordered a corporal to make his way back to Bde. H.Q. to inform them of the serious, not to say desperate, position we were in. I myself picked up a Lewis gun and got off 3 magazines at 400 yards - the gun them jammed. As soon as the high ground North & South of us had been secured, the Bosche in front of us advanced up to the Railway Embankment and lobbed bombs over. Heavy casualties had by this time been sustained from M.G's, Rifles and Bombs. When the L.G. jammed I picked up a rifle and continued to use this till I felt a tap on the shoulder and on looking up, saw a Bosche with rifle and bayonet standing over me.

(sgd) A.C.Clarke
Major.

Copy of letter from Captain H.P.Greaves (Commdg. 178th L.T. Mortar Battery) to Br.-General T.W.Stansfield.

4 Gordon Street,
Burton-on-Trent.

5. 2. 19.

My dear General Stansfield,

I was very pleased to receive your kind and interesting letter of the 2nd inst. and in accordance with your wish I am giving you below a brief and private a/c of the events (as I remember them) of the 21st.

5 a.m. Myton and myself were awakened by the Boche barrage. I immediately gave the "alert". By 6 a.m. my dug-out was completely blown in at the entrance and it took us over 2 hours to dig ourselves out. Judd and Smith-Masters were both down my dug-out at this time. I then went on top - sent down 2 runners to Lieut. Harris (who was in Rly. Reserve) to get definite news as all telephone communication was cut. Our sunken road was very heavily shelled with 5.9's and gas shells. About 9.30 a.m. wounded started to arrive from the front, with garbled a/c's of what was happening. Later 2/Lieut. Hill was brought to my H.Q. badly wounded in the leg and foot. Of his two gun teams, several men had been killed - one gun destroyed by direct hit, and the other he blew up himself. 3 of Harris's guns in Rly. Reserve did some good shooting. When it became evident that "Rly. Reserve" had "gone under", I offered myself, Myton, and some 12 men to Col. Gadd, and of course he accepted us, and put Major Trench and myself in charge of the Sunken road. Shortly after, Trench was killed, only a few yards away from me, in gallantly leading a bombing raid. I immediately reported this fact to Col. Gadd and also told him our flanks were being encircled rapidly. I them tried to carry on in the Sunken Rd, and managed to organize a few firing bays, and for a time we kept the Boche off, although he still crept round our flanks (he came in crowds down the Noreuil Valley). I was then hit in the left thigh by a lump of shrapnel but as it was not very serious I kept on and brought the one Stokes gun I had with me at H.Q. into action. Meanwhile I told Myton to take ½ dozen men (it was all I could spare) and try and guard my right flank (Noreuil Valley). That was the last I saw of Myton and he certainly received no orders from me to go back. Previous to this, thinking we were in for a "thick time" I ordered L/Cpl. Fretwell to take my Stationery box and papers to Bde. H.Q. and report there. I believe he got through alright.

The Boche then started to enfilade the Sunken Rd. with a machine gun from my right. I managed to knock out this M.G. with our last Stokes gun, but lost several men in doing so. By this time our numbers were getting thin, and I deemed it advisable to again acquaint Col. Gadd of the situation, which was then desperate. I therefore went down his dug-out and reported to him and he told me to try and get the men back to the next defence system. I went on top again, and managed to get a few men back. The Boche was rapidly encircling us. He again enfiladed our Sunken Rd. with machine guns, and unfortunately I ran out of Stokes shells, so we destroyed the gun. A few minutes later I was hit by a m.g. bullet through the head, and when the Boche got me I was unconcious (or thereabouts).

I believe Judd (padre) was killed, and Smith-Masters was taken prisoner. Both my subalterns, Hill and Harris, were wounded and taken prisoner. I cannot speak too highly of the courage and coolness displayed by Major Trench.

....

I am, Sir,

Yours very sincerely,

(sgd) H.P.Greaves.

(Capt. Commdg. 178th L.T.Mortar Batt)

178th Brigade.

59th Division.

2/5th BATTALION

NOTTS. & DERBY REGIMENT

APRIL 1918.

Instructions regarding War Diaries and Intelligence Summaries are contained in F. S. Regs., Part II. and the Staff Manual respectively. Title pages will be prepared in manuscript.

1

WAR DIARY
or
~~INTELLIGENCE SUMMARY.~~
(*Erase heading not required.*)

Army Form C. 2118.

2/5 Notts & Derby

Sept 15

2/5TH BATTN. NOTTS & DERBY REGT

Place	Date	Hour	Summary of Events and Information	Remarks and references to Appendices
	1918 April			
CAMBLIGNEUL	1		Marched to AUBIGNY & entrained. Detrained at PROVEN & marched to ST JAN-ter-BIEZEN (Roads Camp). Transport moved by road. Draft of 85 other ranks.	
St JAN-ter-BIEZEN	2		Reorganisation & rest. { Major R. S. PRATT M.C. joined & took over command of Battalion (posted as 2/c)	
		5 pm	{ 2/Lt M.D. BARROWS posted as Adjutant. Captain C.N. Littleboy, M.C rejoined from Brigade staff & took over command of C. Company	
		11 pm	Draft of 71 other ranks	
	3		Reorganisation & training	
		3 pm	Inspection by General PLUMMER, G.O.C II Army, who gave a short discourse to all officers on general situation	
		5 pm	Draft of 21 other ranks	
	4		General Training. Brigade Commander addressed recently joined drafts.	
	5		" " All Lewis Guns tested & fired	
	6		" " Draft of 85 other ranks.	
	7	10 am	Parade & march to WINNEZEELE Area. Billeted in scattered farms. A good march	See Appx "A"
WINNEZEELE Area	8		Battalion parade & general Training	
	9		" " "	

A6945 Wt. W11422/M1160 350,000 12/16 D. D. & L. Forms/C./2118/14.

Instructions regarding War Diaries and Intelligence Summaries are contained in F. S. Regs., Part II. and the Staff Manual respectively. Title pages will be prepared in manuscript.

2

WAR DIARY

or

~~INTELLIGENCE~~ SUMMARY.

(*Erase heading not required.*)

Army Form C. 2118.

Place	Date	Hour	Summary of Events and Information	Remarks and references to Appendices
	April			
WINNEZEELE Area	10	10am	Orders received to prepare for move	[illegible]
		12.45pm 1pm	B Company moved by march to WINNEZEELE to entrain Remainder to WINNEZEELE to ~~entrain at~~ ~~[illegible]~~ ~~2.25pm~~	
		6.45pm 8.30pm	Entrained Detrained at CHEESEMARKET, POPERINGHE, marched to ST LAWRENCE Camp (BRANDHOEK Area) G.11.c (Transport by road)	
BRANDHOEK Area	11		General Training.	
	12	12noon	Orders to move.. Major J.C. BAINES arrived & took over command of the battalion.	JCB
		3.35pm	Entrained at BRANDHOEK in 3 trains Detrained at LA CLYTTE & marched toward KEMMEL	
			Brigade Commander met by C.O. at N.20.b.8.6. & informs him the Brigade may relieve the S. Africans near WHYTSCHAETE	JCB
			No orders received, & battalion bivouacked in field off LA CLYTTE - KEMMEL RD (1st Line Transport brought up & returned to near WESTOUTRE)	JCB
KEMMEL	13	7.20am	Orders received to move battalion to fill gap reported in line at T11 central to T10a	JCB
		7.45am	Moved off & halted at LINDENHOEK X Roads. Orders issued to 2 Companies (A & C) to fill gap. 2 Companies in reserve (B & D) & HQ moved up to railway.	JCB
		11am	A & C Companies filled gap. In touch on flanks & incorporated 90th Field Coy. R.E. in line. On right reports showed touch with WORCESTERS, & left with 9th R.I.F.	JCB
			Line held just S.E. of WULVERGHEM - NEUVE EGLISE Road. Enemy holding ridge in T.11. central & T10 central with M.Gs.	JCB
		1.55pm	Casualties inflicted on enemy, who appeared to be digging about T11d70. Enemy MG & sniping.	JCB
		4pm	Right flank extended as ordered to ARMY line to relieve one Company of WORCESTERS. Touch established with GLOUCESTERS after extension	JCB

A6945 Wt. W11422/M1160 350,000 12/16 D. D. & L. Forms/C./2118/14.

Instructions regarding War Diaries and Intelligence Summaries are contained in F. S. Regs., Par. II. and the Staff Manual respectively. Title pages will be prepared in manuscript.

3

Army Form C. 2118.

WAR DIARY
or
~~INTELLIGENCE SUMMARY.~~
(Erase heading not required.)

2/5th BATTN. NOTTS & DERBY REGT.

Place	Date	Hour	Summary of Events and Information	Remarks and references to Appendices
	April			
KEMMEL	13	5pm 6.30pm	Heavy shelling round HQ. 40 casualties.	JHB
(HQ in railway)			Two E.A. at 2000ft driven off by our fire (M.G. & rifle) Patrolling all night, no information gained. Ridge through T11 central & 10 d shelled by our artillery.	JHB
	14	7.30am	Shelling started & continued all day in varying intensity Neuve Eglise captured by enemy & retaken by counter attack.	JHB
		11.20am	Battalion obtained harassing fire on our front from our artillery	
		11.25am	1 Company 2/6 Sherwood Foresters came into line on right & connected with SHROPSHIRES	JHB
		1pm	Enemy attacked our front line. 50 enemy advanced on left Company (C) 100x stopped by L.G. fire. About 20 advanced on ~~left~~ right company & were held. Enemy retired & appeared to be digging in	JHB
		3pm	Situation normal. Captain QUIBELL wounded	JHB
		4.30pm	Orders received to move support companies into trenches in T4 when quiet Shelling again heavy	JHB
		5.30pm	Support companies ordered to move into line of trenches T3 b 5.8 to T4 b 9.1	JHB
		6.0pm	Enemy broke through NEUVE EGLISE	
		7.50pm	C (left) still in T10 b & 11a A (right) doubtful	JHB
		8.0pm	Battalion HQ at N32 b 7.9 & support Companies in position. 2/6 Sher For. on right Front Companies drew back but advanced on to original line	JHB
(HQ N32 b 7.9)		11.30pm	Order received for front Companies to withdraw at 1.30am to KINGSWAY Trench in T34 & 35 — front line to be T4 a 0.3 to T5 a ~~[illegible]~~ 3.2. Orders issued by runner to companies for this move	JHB
	15	6.0am	Move completed. Report from D that A & C passed through his line at 4.25am 4.28am	JHB
		7.35am	Front line enfiladed from east by shell fire & MG	JHB

A6945 Wt. W11422/M1160 350,000 12/16 D. D. & L. Forms/C./2118/14.

Army Form C. 2118.

Instructions regarding War Diaries and Intelligence Summaries are contained in F. S. Regs., Part II. and the Staff Manual respectively. Title pages will be prepared in manuscript.

4

WAR DIARY
or
~~INTELLIGENCE~~ SUMMARY.
(*Erase heading not required.*)

Place	Date	Hour	Summary of Events and Information	Remarks and references to Appendices
	April			
KEMMEL	15		Touch was not gained with 108th Inf. Bde on left: one company of the 7th Sherwood Foresters was employed to fill this gap.	JB
			The support line in KINGSWAY also failed to get into touch with 108th Bde for some time, but eventually succeeded.	JB
		8.15 am	Message received that 108th Bde had been pushed in in Dgc. The left companies of front & support line ordered to form a defensive flank	JB
			Shelling severe all day. Enemy O.B (with perfect observation) up near WULVERGHEM	JB
		1 pm	D Coy (left front) reported situation serious, only 40 men left line being continuously & heavily shelled. 2 platoons A ordered up to support & stiffen line	JB
		1.15 pm 2.??pm	Enemy working forward singly for attack or to form a line Situation quiet defensive flanks formed	JB
		8.0 pm	C ordered to attack ELBOW Farm which was reported occupied. Action taken & farm found to be unoccupied.	JB
		9.30 pm	Orders received to withdraw into reserve through Army lines. Orders issued & a difficult operation successfully carried out owing to energy and excellent leading of Company Officers.	JB
	16	3.0 am 5.0 am	HQ withdrawn & established at N.25 b.91 All companies rendez-vous round Xroads at N.19c	JB
			Gas shelling & heavy shells most of the morning	JB
		8. am	Company commanders assembled at HQ & all arrangements made for counter-attack, for reinforcing, & for forming a defensive flank.	JB
			A Coy located at H25.d.3.5 watching front across H31b B in N25c97 ready for defensive flank along spur in 25c D in trench N25b2.3 to support A. C at farm N25b37 watching H32.	JB
		8.30 pm	5 officer reinforcements arrive – night quiet.	JB
	17	4.30 am	Shelling commenced.	JB

A6945 Wt. W11422/M1160 350,000 12/16 D. D. & L. Forms/C./2118/14.

Instructions regarding War Diaries and Intelligence Summaries are contained in F. S. Regs., Par. II. and the Staff Manual respectively. Title pages will be prepared in manuscript.

5

WAR DIARY
or
~~INTELLIGENCE SUMMARY.~~
(Erase heading not required.)

Army Form C. 2118.

Place	Date	Hour	Summary of Events and Information	Remarks and references to Appendices
			2/8th BATTn. NOTTS & DERBY REGT.	
	April			
KEMMEL	17		Attack developed on front & right flanks. Front line held firm. Right flank gave a little where mixed units were holding it on N 31 a 76 to right of LANCS FUS	JHB
		10 45	A ordered to be ready for counter-attack B moved to defensive flank D " up to support A	JHB
		3.0pm	Patrol under Lt PALMER established touch with 1st LEICESTERS at N 31 a 05. Officers from 177 Inf Bde came up to study situation	JHB
		3.15pm	99th Inf Regt, 28th Bwn. FRENCH, arrived	
		4.45pm	Gap reported in front line from N 31 a 05 to N 31 b 05. A Company fill this. D moved up in support & C into D's position. Gap taken over by French & all companies of this Battalion returned to old positions Night quiet	JHB
	18	4.30am 7.30am	Heavy bombardment. French patrolled into DONEGAL Farm & took prisoners Touch gained with 1st LEICESTERS again N 31 a 46. 9th R I F came up in support on hill.	JHB
			Lancs. Fusiliers reported enemy advancing in fifties & hundreds on DONEGAL S.O.S obtained by pigeon.	
		8.25am	A & D ordered to counter attack if required	JHB
		11.0am	French G.O.C. reported front line to W of DONEGAL penetrated & asked for two companies to counter attack. A & D ordered accordingly. R.I.F warned to support if required	JHB
		11.20am	French G.O.C. now states he does not want these two companies to go beyond support line & to remain in observation there. Request complied with	JHB
see next page X →		12.45pm	Hun reported concentrating but no further attack developed Verbal orders for relief received from Brigade Major	JHB
	19	4.30am	All arrangements made. Last Company relieved, HQ left KEMMEL.	JHB see Appx "B"

A6945 Wt. W11422/M1160 350,000 12/16 D. D. & L. Forms/C./2118/14.

Instructions regarding War Diaries and Intelligence Summaries are contained in F. S. Regs., Part II. and the Staff Manual respectively. Title pages will be prepared in manuscript.

6

WAR DIARY
or
~~INTELLIGENCE SUMMARY.~~
(Erase heading not required.)

Army Form C. 2118.

2/5th BATTn. NOTTS & DERBY REGT.

Place	Date	Hour	Summary of Events and Information	Remarks and references to Appendices
	April			
KEMMEL	19		Battalion marched out to farm just clear of WESTOUTRE where Transport ~~was~~ [on previous page was]. Total casualties KILLED 1 off 32 O.R. D of W. 3 O.R. wounded 3 off 135 O.R. Missing 30 O.R.	JHB
	X [place]	4.20pm	Situation :- WEST YORKS N 25 d 0.2 – N 25 d 31 Right of LANES. FUS at N 32 a 44. French left at N 31 b 85.05. {Gap well covered & patrolled {BEAVER not occupied.	JHB
WESTOUTRE	20		Entrained at HEKSKEN for DIRTY BUCKET Camp, N of BRANDHOEK. (Transport by road)	JHB
BRANDHOEK Area	21	11am	Marched from BRANDHOEK to HOUTKERQUE (10 miles) SHRINE Camp	JHB
	22 23 24		Rest & training Draft of 12 officers, 81 O.R. arrived.	JHB
	25		Digging on WATOU - CAESTRE line.	JHB
	26		Sudden move to ROADS Camp, St JAN-ter-BIEZEN. In Div! reserve	JHB
St JAN-ter BIEZEN	27 28		Standing-to & training.	JHB
	29		Return by march to HOUTKERQUE.	JHB See appx "C"
HOUTKERQUE	30		General Training.	JHB
			Strength 1/4/18: 11. Off. 341. O.R.	
			" 30/4/18: 25. Off. 744. O.R.	

ORDERLY ROOM 30/4/18. 2/5th Battn. Notts & Derby Regt.

JH Barnes Lt. Col.
Cdg
2/5th BATTn. NOTTS & DERBY REGT.

A6945 Wt. W11422/M1160 35,000 12/16 D. D. & L. Forms/C./2118/14.

War Diary

"A" Copy No. 14

OPERATION ORDERS No. 1

by

Major R.S. PRATT M.C.,

commanding

2/5th. Battalion, The Sherwood Foresters.

.... 6.8.1918.

Reference Map Sheet 27 1/40,000.

1. INTENTION. The Battalion will march to K 25.c.8.8. to-morrow.

2. INSTRUCTIONS. (a) The Battalion will parade in Mass on the Football ground ready to move off at 9.50 a.m.
Dress - Full Marching Order. Soft Caps will be worn.
Markers will report to R.S.M. at 9.40 a.m. H.Qrs. will parade on right of Battalion and Drums on right of H.Qrs.
(b) Route. WATOU - Road junction K.4.d.5.6. - ST LAURENT.
(c) Order of March. H.Qrs. "A", "B", "C", "D" Coys. at 100 yards interval.
(d) Baggage All blankets (tightly rolled in bundles of 10) Officers' Kits, Rifles and packs of the Band will be dumped in empty cook-house by Battalion Orderly Room (recently used by H.G.C.) at 8.30 a.m. Company Lewis Gun Limbers to be loaded in park by 9.15 a.m.
(e) Reveille :- 6.0 a.m. Breakfast 7.30 a.m.
Sick parade 7 a.m.
(f) Billets. A billeting party of two men per Coy. and Headquarters Coy., under R.Q.M.Sgt. WARD will parade at Bn. Orderly Room at 7.15 a.m. (see c)
(g) Slow Party. Men recommended by M.O./will parade under Corpl. Dean at Battalion Orderly Room at 9.40 a.m. All men who fall out must have written leave signed by O.C. Company, and must join slow party.
(h) Camp. The whole camp will be left absolutely clean. Camp Inspection 9.30 a.m.

3. TRANSPORT. Officers' Mounts will be in camp at 9.45 a.m. The Officers' Mess Cart at Mess at 8.45 a.m. Maltese Cart will report to the M.O. at 8.30 a.m. 2 pairs of horses will report to Quartermaster at 9.30 a.m. to draw wagons up singly from the park.
All transport to be ready to move (wagons hitched in in Park) by 10 a.m., and to follow Battalion ... 100 yards in rear of Company.

4. REPORTS To head of column.

5. ACKNOWLEDGE.

Issued at 12.15 a.m.

M D Barrows.
2nd. Lieutenant and Adjutant
2/5th. Battalion, The Sherwood Foresters.

DISTRIBUTION.

Copy No.
1 Commanding Officer.
2 2nd. in command
3 Adjutant
4 "A" Coy.
5 "B" Coy.
6 "C" Coy.
7 "D" Coy.
8 H.Q.Coy.
9 Quartermaster
10 Transport Officer
11 R.S.M.
12 Medical Officer
13 R.S.M.
14 File
15 and 16 War Diary.

B

2/5th Battalion THE SHERWOOD FORESTERS

Narrative of operations 12th - 18th April 1918.

12.4.18. The Battalion entrained at BRANDHOEK at 3.35 p.m. for LA CLYTTE, and on arrival marched towards KEMMEL. The Commanding Officer went on to meet the Brigadier just outside KEMMEL.

Nothing definate could be learned except a report that we might be called upon to relieve the South African Brigade in the line near WHYTSCHAETE.

Eventually the Battalion bivouched just off the road. Cookers were sent for, and all made as comfortable as possible under the circumstances There was shelling during the night, but no harm done to us .

13.4.18. At 7.20 a.m. orders were received from Brigade to move, and fill a gap in the line that was reported to exist between T.11. central and T. 10.a., and to be prepared to attack if required.

The Battalion moved at 7.45 a.m. The Commanding Officer going on to get more particulars from the Brigader. The Battalion halted at the LINDENHOEK Cross Roads, and all officers met, and orders were issued.

"A" and "C" Companies were to move down the road to the railway crossing, and then to move in artillery formation covered by a screen to fill the gap, Lieut. Palmer being sent on with a patrol to learn the exact situation.

Headquarters moved down the road, aand were established at railway crossing in a small dug-out "B" and "D" Companies were placed along the railway and dug themselves in.

"A" and "C" Companies successfully got into position by 11 a.m.(with 7 casualties from Machine Gun fire ,and snipers) and were in touch on right and left just S.E. of WOLVERGHEM - NEUVE -EGLISE Road, but could not get to the ridge as it was held by the enemy, and machine guns.

Plenty of hostile movement observed which was fired on, and casualties inflicted.

At 4 p.m. the Battalion was ordered to extend the right flank, to relieve a company of WORCESTERS and did so, linking up with the GLOUCESTERS. About 5 o'clock, the shelling became very heavy, chiefly enfilading. Headquarters and the two support Companies from the MESSINES RIDGE, and about 40 casualties were inflicted

Many of the men had not been under fire before, and it was severe trial to them, as the shelling was of heavy calibre. However the men stood it in a wonderful manner.

Towards dusk one enemy plane flew very low over our front line.

14.4.8. Hostile shelling started at 7.30 a.m. Various reports keep coming in about NEUVE- EGLISE ; stragglers came down the road, but were rallied and sent back.

A counter attack from our right restored the NEUVE- EGLISE position. At 1120 a.m. the enemy were reported concentrating opposite our front, and harassing fire was opened by our artillery

SHEET No. 2.

One Company of the 2/6th Sherwood Foresters went up to strengthen our right, and put one platoon in the line, and kept three in close support.

Later about 1 p.m. the enemy started to attack in not very great strength, and was stopped by our fire. He withdrew and appeared to be digging in along the LEBURK FARM Ridge

Captain Quibell was wounded in the afternoon, and Lieut. Ford gassed. Captain Clifford took over command of "D" Company.

The hostile shelling grew very heavy again about 4.30 p.m.

We were ordered to sideslip with one of the support companies eastward, as the 2/6 Sherwood Foresters had taken their position, and decided to move both the support companies into trenches in T.3.b.5.8 and T.4.b. 9.1. as at present they were in rather an exposed situation

At 6 p.m. the enemy captured NEUVE-EGLISE.

Our front line was still in position, and in conjunction with C.O. 2/6th Sherwood Foresters

We established a joint Headquarters with the GLOUCESTERS at NW33.d.3.0.

By 8 p.m. the two support companies were in position, passing through heavy shelling in getting there, and suffering casualties.

Captain Clifford being wounded two officers from the 7th Sherwood Foresters reported. Lieut Spatcher being sent to command "A" Company and Lieut. Green taking over "D" Company from Captain Clifford.

Battalion Headquarters were finally established at H.32.b.7.9.

At 1130 p.m. C.O. 2/6th Sherwood Foresters brought me orders that the front line companies were to withdraw through support line to KINGSWAY TRENCH in T.34 and 35, the original support line thus becoming front line from T.4.a. 0.3. to T.5.a.3.2. Orders were sent out by runners

The difficult operation of front companies withdrawing was successfully carried out, but was rather late.

At one point in the roadside the Commanding Officer met Cpl. Mosby of "A" Company, and informed him of the situation, and he took orders to "A" Coy which helped largely in making matters clear.

15.4.18.

The movement was completed by 6 a.m. "A" Coy passing through "D" Company at 4.25 am and "C" Coy at 4.20 am.

Our new front line was enfiladed by hostile artillery from MESSINES.

Touch with the 108th Infantry Brigade on the left was never quite gained, and a company of the 7th Sherwood Foresters moved up to fill the gap.. Complete touch was made with the 2/6th Sherwood Foresters on our right, dug in W. of railway. About 8.15 a.m. a telephone message was received telling us that the 108th Brigade had been pushed in about D.29.C.

Orders were at once issued for companies of front & support lines to form a defensive flank.

Shelling continued heavy all day on the front line and the enemy had a balloon up over WULVERGHEM way, and had complete observation of any movement.

"D" Company lost men steadily, and finally were reduced to about 40 strong, so two platoons of "A" Coy went up in support

Single men were seen working forward either to form a line, or preparatory for an assult.

Lieut Palmer had a forward Headquarters at head of buried cable near DAYLIGHT CORNER, and rendered invaluable service in getting messages through quickly.

At 3 p.m. a message was received from Brigade that the enemy were in ELBOW FARM. "C" Company attacked with a platoon, but report was incorrect.

At 9.30 p.m. orders were received to withdraw from previous position, and pass into Brigade reserve N. of KEMMEL.

Once again owing to the darkness and ignorance of the country, this was a most difficult operation and was only successfully concluded by the energy and initiative of the Company Commanders, and the excellent arrangements made by the Brigade for the guides. Throughout the day "D" Company inflicted heavy casualties on the enemy by Lewis Gun and rifle fire.

16.4.18.

Battalion Headquarters withdrew at 3 a.m. and established again at H.25.b. 19.1.

The Companies all rendesvouzed around Cross Roads in H. 19.c. by 5 a.m., and settled down in scattered groups. Gas shelling and ordinary shelling was fairly heavy Lieut. Cook being killed.

The battalion was warned to be ready for counter attack or reinforcing as the situation demanded, and the four Company Commanders came to Headquarters and all arrangements were made and verbal orders issued. The Companies moved about a little to avoid shelling but were arranged in echelon.

17.418

Enemy started shelling early Report came in that both flanks of the 7th Sherwood Foresters were penitrated. A Lancashire Fusilier Officer reported heavy attack on the right, and asked for reinforcements. All wires were cut to Brigade

Our right flank was always obscure beyond the Lancashire Fusiliers, and was apparently held by a few West Yorks joining up with the VIII Corps Schools

The situation was vauge, and it was difficult to judge as to the correctness of the reports. However as the left seemed safe, action was taken on the right flank, which embraced the reentering valleys of the S.W. slopes of KEMMEL HILL, which always appeared to be the danger spot.

"A" Company moved up to counter attack if required "D" Company in support "B" Company formed a defensive flank and "C" Company held a watching brief.

An officers patrol under Lieut Palmer went out, and gained touch with the 1st Leicesters, who also were perturbed about the area which was engaging our attention

Situation remained normal, but required watching.

At 3.15 p.m. the 99th Infantry Regt. 28th Division French Army arrived on the scene

Once again a gap was reported at 4.45 p.m. in the same area. "A" Company filled this, and our other Companies all moved one up

Later in the day the French took over this gap, and I withdrew "A" Company and ~~established~~ echeloned the others backwards again

The night generally was quiet.

18.4.18. At 4.30 a.m. an intense bombardment started, which lasted about two hours. The French patrolled into DONEGOL FARM, killed some enemy and made some prisoners

Touch was made again with the 1st Leicesters by Major Pratt, who had extended to their left.

SHEET No. 4.

The 9th R,I.F. came up in support to us early in the morning, and were placed near the Windmill. Lancs. Fusiliers reported strong enemy attack from DONEGAL FARM
S.O.S. was obtained by use of pigeons.
At 11 O'clock French Regimental Commander reported to me that the line W of DONEGAL FARM had been penitrated and asked for immediate counter attack. "A" and "D" Companies ordered to attack. 9th R.I.F. warned to keep in touch, and help if required
Directly afterwards he stated he only wanted them to occupy support trenches. Orders were ammended accordingly, and "A" and "D" Companies accupied trenches as ordered
At 12.45 a.m. the enemy was again reported massing, but no attack developed
The Brigade Major came up and told me we were being relieved that night.
All preliminary arrangements were made. Owing to the difficulty of making the French understand the situation, the relief was slow and difficult, and it was 4.15 a.m. on the 19th before the last Company got away, and 4.30 a.m. before Headquarters left
It was just daylight, but the Battalion got out safely and went to the Transport Lines N. of WESTOUTRE.

Secret "C"

Operation Orders No 2

by

Lt-Col. A. C. Baines.

Comdg 2/5th Bn Sherwood Foresters

28-4-18.

Reference. Sheet 27

1. Intention The Battalion will march tomorrow to Houtkerque Route E 29 B - E 22 A.

2. Instructions

(a). Companies will pass B. O R as follows

Headquarters, B + D	8-54 a M
Drums + A	8-56 a M
C	8-58 a M
Transport	9-0 a M

Dress - Full marching order. Steel Helmets.

L. G. Limbers to be loaded by 7-45 a M.

Officers' valises on Wagons
by 7-30 AM
Mess cart & Maltese cart to
be loaded by 8-20 a M.
Officers mounts in camp
by 8-40 a M

(c). Advance Party
1 NCO per company + HQ
will report to Lt Palmer
at B.O.R. at 8-20 a M
with company strengths
They will proceed as an
advance party.

3. Routine.
Reveille 6-0 a M
Breakfast 6-30 a M
Sick Parade 7-0 a M
Dinner after arrival in Camp

4 Acknowledge

Issued at 10-45 pm

M D Barrows
Capt & Adj

Distribution

Copy No. 1. C.O.
2 2nd i/c.
3 O.C. A Coy
4 O.C. B.
5 O.C. C
6 O.C. D.
7. R.S.M. & HQ
8 Lt. Palmer
9 M.O.
10 T.O.
11 Q.M.
12 Adjutant.
13 File
14 } War Diary.
15 }

Capt. & Adjutant.

Instructions regarding War Diaries and Intelligence Summaries are contained in F. S. Regs., Part II. and the Staff Manual respectively. Title pages will be prepared in manuscript.

WAR DIARY
or
~~INTELLIGENCE SUMMARY.~~
(Erase heading not required.)

Army Form C. 2118.

2/5 Vol 16

Place	Date 1918	Hour	Summary of Events and Information	Remarks and references to Appendices
	MAY		2/5th BATTn. NOTTS & DERBY REGT.	
HOUTKERQUE	1		Dull cold day Training: Lewis Gunners on Range & 8 picked shots per Company as snipers. Football in afternoon. Orders received to march to K.17.a to dig a line of trenches from WATOU to ABEELE.	
	2		Dull day. Advance party under Lt Lewis move off 8 am: "A" Coy 10 am to pitch tents for battalion. Remainder of Battalion, 2.0 pm. QM Stores & bulk of transport did not move.	See Op. Orders No 3 attached
	3		Fine day. C.O. & Company Commanders reconnoitre work. Training in morning. Digging from 1 pm to 6 pm	
	4		Heavy counter-preparation heard at 4.30 am. Fine day. Short ceremonial parade; & digging from 12 noon. Return about 5 pm.	
	5		Moved by march at 7.50 am to near WATOU. Embussed there, & proceeded to ST OMER. Transport by road. (Sudden orders) Battalion billeted in French barracks.	
ST OMER	6		Battalion disbanded. Rolls etc. prepared all day. Transport arrived at noon. The Brigade Commander addressed battalion in barrack square	
	7.		G.O.C. 59th Division addressed battalion. At 5.0 pm 15 officers +560 O.R. marched to St OMER Station & entrained for Base, Calais	
	8.		Clearing up	
	9		Battalion Training Staff & Transport left ST OMER at 7.46 am, & marched to BLESSY (14 miles) arriving 1.0 pm. Billeted in village.	See Op Orders No 4
BLESSY	10.		Marched to BOURS (14 miles) & billeted in village	No 5 attached

(A7092). Wt. W12839/M1293. 75,000. 1/17. D. D. & L., Ltd. Forms/C.2118/14.

Instructions regarding War Diaries and Intelligence Summaries are contained in F. S. Regs., Part II. and the Staff Manual respectively. Title pages will be prepared in manuscript.

WAR DIARY

~~or~~

~~INTELLIGENCE SUMMARY.~~

(*Erase heading not required.*)

Army Form C. 2118.

Place	Date	Hour	Summary of Events and Information	Remarks and references to Appendices
	MAY		2/5th BATTn. NOTTS & DERBY REGT.	
BOURS	11 to 13		At BOURS	
	14		4 Company Commanders & QM sent to AUCHEL to be attached to 11th (Garrison Guard) Bn Royal Scotch Fusiliers to instruct in duties. This unit engaged in digging a trench system.	
	15		Transport under 2/Lt H. R. Spendlove leave for ETAPLES (Concentration Camp) & are struck off strength. C.O., 2/c, & I.O inspected line nr BARLIN for position for a Division	
	16 to 18		Ordinary Training. Very hot weather	
	19		One officer sent to 2nd (G.G) Bn Royal Irish Regt at HURIONVILLE	
	20		Inoculation for Training Staff. {Capt NAYLOR & two instructors (& afterwards 1 CQMS) sent to Div L.G. School as staff	
	21		ditto	
	22		Firing practices.	
	23 to 30		Training (27th - 28th on range). Officers visit G.G battalions at intervals. Orders received to be ready to join 16th Division.	
			Strength May 1st 25 Off 738 O.R. May 31st 11 " 72 "	

[signature] Lt. Col.
Cdg 2/5th Battn The Sherwood Foresters.

(A7092). Wt. W12839/M1293. 750,000. 1/17. D. D. & L., Ltd. Forms/C.2118/14.

SECRET. Copy No. 14....

2/5th. Battalion, The Sherwood Foresters ORDER No. 3

Refernce Sheet 27 N.E. 1.5.1918.

1. The Battalion will march tomorrow to area K 17.a. (about 3 miles) ROUTE :- WATOU - Destina tion.

2, (a) Reveille 6.45 a.m. Breakfast 7,30 a.m.
Sick Parade 8.0 a.m. Dinners 12.30 p.m.

(b) Tents. Companies will arrange for a party to be at each tent at 8.45 a.m. The R.S.M. will arrange that parties are ready at all tents not in Company Lines. At 8.45 a.m. the Regimental Call will be blown on the Bugle, when all tents will be struck.

They will be dumped in space opposite Companies' Mess Hut by 9 a.m.

(c) Advance Party. One N.C.O. per Company, Headquarters and Transport will parade under Lieut, L. E. Lewis at Battalion Orderly Room at 8.0 a.m . as an advance party.

Lieut. Lewis will proceed t o K 16 b.8.8., and will arrange guides for the advance Company and for the Battalion.

(d) Parades. "A" Company will parade at 10 a.m., and will march to the new area in advance to pitch tents.

The Battalion less "A" Company and Transport, will be formed up ready to move off at 1.55 P.m.

Markers to report to R.S.M. at 1.45 p.m.

(e) Transport. The Transportwill move under Brigade arrangements after the Battalion has cleared the Camp.

One lorry will report at 9.0 a.m. to convey tents to new area. The R.S.M. will arr ange for loading party.

One lorry will report to comvey blankets, and can be used as often as required.

Blankets to be dumped at Qu artermaster's Stores by 10.30 a.m. Officers' kits,and rifles and packs of the Dand by 12.30 p.m. All other s urplus kit 11.30 a.m.

Mess Cart will be loaded at Company Mess Hut by 1.15 p.m.

Maltese cart to be loaded b y 12.30 p.m.

Officers' horses in camp by 1.45 p.m.

3, Acknowledge.

N W Barrows

Captain and Adjutant,
2/5th. Battalion, Theb Sherwood Foresters

Issued at 11 p.m.

DISTRIBUTION.

Copy No,	
1	Commanding Officer.
2	2nd. in Command.
3	Adjutant.
4	"A" Company.
5	"B" Company.
6	"C" Company.
7	"D" Company.
8	R.S.M. and Headquarters.
9	Quartermaster
10	Transport Officer.
11	Medical Officer.
12	Lieutenant Lewis.
13	File
14 & 15	War Diary.

Copy No.......5

2/5th. Battalion, The Sherwood Foresters ORDER No. 4

Reference Map HAZEBROUCK May 6th. 1918.

1. The Battalion Training Staff, plus Transport, will move to MAMETZ Sub-area tomorrow by march.

2. Instructions. Breakfast 6.30 a.m. Parade ready to move off 7.50 a.m. DRESS Drill Order with haversacks and water bottles, soft caps.
All members of the Battalion Training Staff and attached will parade under their own C.S.M. Transport to be hitched in at same time.

Transport. Mess Cart to be at Mess at 7 a.m.
Company Lewis Gun Limbers to be loaded with packs (all B.T.S. with Companies) by 7.40 a.m.
Officers' Kits to be loaded by servants, under the supervision of the Quartermaster by 7.20 a.m. on to Baggage wagon. Officers' Mounts to be at Mess at 7.40 a.m. The Quartermaster will arrange that one cooker cooks while on themarch.
Dinners On arrival.

3 Battalion Training Staff Ord. Sergt. Sergt. Cresswell JF

M D Barrows
Captain and Adjutant,
2/5th. Battalion, The Sherwood Foresters.

Issued at 11.15 p.m.

DISTRIBUTION.

Copy No. 1 Headquarters
2 Quartermaster and Transport Officer.
3 R.S.M.
4 All Companies.
5 & 6 War Diary .

SECRET,

2/5th. Battn Sherwood Foresters After Order No. 4

May 8th.1918,

1.ROUTE. ARCQUES + BELLECROIX -ROQUETOIRE - MAMETZ - BLESSY.

2.TIMES. All times stated in Operation No.4 will be 15 minutes earlier, and n ot as stated.

3,ADVANCE PARTY. Lieut. L.E. Lewis and one mounted orderly for Tramsport will meet the Staff Captain at the Church,REBECQ at 9,0 a.m. Transport Officer will arrange for mounted orderly to report to Lieut, Lewis at the Mess at 7.50 a.m.

4, Acknowledge this and operation Order No.4 at the same time.

N W Barrows
Captain and Adjutant,
2/5th. Battalion, Sherwood Foresters.

Issued at 11.30 p.m.

DISTRIBUTION.

Copy No,1 Headquarters.
2 Q.M. & T.O.
3 R.S.M.
4 All Companies.
5 & 6 War Diary.

SECRET. Copy No. 9.

2/5th. Battalion, Sherwood Foresters ORDER No. 5

Reference SheetsLENS 11 andHAZEBROUCK 5a. May 9th. 1918.

1. The Battalion Transing staff plu s Transport will march to BOURS tomorrow (14 miles).

2. Starting Point :- Headquarters Mess,BLESSY.

3. ROUTE :- ESTREE-BLAMCHE - RELY - AUCHY-AU-BOIS - NEDONCHELLE - PERNES.

4 The column will pass starting point at 8,15 a.m. Order of march as for today.

5. Lieut, Lewis, R.Q.M.Sgt. Ward, and a Mounted Orderly for Transport will leave the Starting Point at 8.0 a,m. and proceed to meet the Staff Captain at the Church,BOURS.

6. Instructions :-
(a) Trnasport. A G.S. Wagon will be at Headquarters Mess by 7.30 am. All Officers' kits will be loaded on this by 7.40 a.m. One Limber will report to Battalion Training Staff Orderly Sergeant at No.22 Billet at 7.30 a.m. All packs will be loaded on this from No. 21 and 22 billets by 7.45 a.m.
One limber will report to Battalion Training Staff Orderly Sergeant at No. 17 billet a t 7.30 a.m. All packs will be loaded on this from No. 17 billet and No. 19 billet, plus Orderly Room Stores, by 7.45 a.m.
(b) Routine :- Breakfast 7 a.m. Dinners as to-day. Dress :- As to-day. (Haversacks to be worn at the side),

7. ACKNOWLEDGE.

M D Barrows
Captain and Adjutant,
2/5th. Battalion, The Sherwood Foresters.

Issued at 6.45 p.m.

DISTRIBUTION.

Copy No.	
1	Headquarters.
2	Q.M. And T.O.
3	R.S.M.
4,5,6 and 7	All Companies.
8	File
9 & 10	War Diary.

Instructions regarding War Diaries and Intelligence Summaries are contained in F. S. Regs., Part II. and the Staff Manual respectively. Title pages will be prepared in manuscript.

WAR DIARY
or
~~INTELLIGENCE SUMMARY.~~
(Erase heading not required.)

Army Form C. 2118.

36

Vol 17

Place	Date	Hour	Summary of Events and Information	Remarks and references to Appendices
	1918			
	JUNE		2/5th Sherwood Foresters.	
BOURS	1		Training	
	2		Very hot day. Move to PREURES by bus - Transport by road. Left BOURS 10 am. Arrived PREURES 2.30pm. Training Staff attd 49th Inf. Bde; 16th (Irish) Division.	See Orders 6
PREURES	3		Training	
	4		Training and reports on accommodation & training facilities in area for 80th American Div.	
	5 & 6		Training - very fine days	
	7		Moved to HUMBERT & back to PREURES same day	See Orders No 7
	8 & 9		8th Interior Economy & 9th training again.	
	10		Move to BEZINGHEM, & attached 47th Inf. Bde.	See Orders No 8
	11		Billeted for Americans & explored Training Area	
BEZINGHEM	12 & 13		Training	
	14		Tactical Scheme. C.O proceeds on leave to U.K. Capt R.S PRATT M.C. commands	
	15		General Training. Arrange water tanks for Americans.	
	16		16 Div ordered to England to be made up to strength. 317th American Inf Regt detrained at SAMER - 2nd Battalion arrive at BEZINGHEM 9.0pm. Orders to move to HALINGHEN area.	
	17		Orders re HALINGHEN cancelled. 16th Div left area for Boulogne & England. 34th Div. take over. Arranged for schools for 2nd Bn, 317th Inf Regt (A)	
	18		Schools commenced, & general supervision of Americans.	
	19		All previous orders cancelled. Affiliation ordered thus:- HQ — HQ 317th Inf Regt D Coy - 1st Bn " " B " 2nd " " C " 3rd " " A HQ Coy, 317th Inf Regt	
	20		Affiliation carried out. Regtl School commenced. Lewis Gunners 8 N.C.Os per Bn under Captain Drysdale. Bombers 12 NCOs per Bn under Lt Lewis (4 day courses for both)	

D. D. & L., London, E.C.
(A8094) Wt. W1771/M2031 750,000 5/17 Sch. 52 Forms/C2118/14

Instructions regarding War Diaries and Intelligence Summaries are contained in F. S. Regs., Part II. and the Staff Manual respectively. Title pages will be prepared in manuscript.

Army Form C. 2118.

WAR DIARY
or
~~INTELLIGENCE SUMMARY.~~
(Erase heading not required.)

Place	Date	Hour	Summary of Events and Information	Remarks and references to Appendices
	JUNE		2/5th Sherwood Foresters	
BEZINGHEM	21 to 27		General Training of Americans. Our instructors had as holidays Sundays & such days as Americans did Tactical Schemes. A cricket ground was secured & matting laid down but was abandoned later	JCB
	28		34th Div relieved by 39th Div. 117th Bde administers SAMER area.	JCB
	29		Americans reviewed by H.R.H. Duke of Connaught.	JCB
	30		Sunday.	
			Strength June 1 11 off 71 OR " 30 10 " 51 "	
		No	LIST OF Honours awarded during Month for action 12 – 19 April	
		(1)	D.S.O. Lt. Col. J. C. BAINES.	JCB
		(4)	M.C. T/Lt G. C Cossar, (Att^d) R.A.M.C 2/Lt A/Capt J. N. Jacques 2/Lt N. F. Spatcher (Att^d) 7th Sher. Fors. Lieut. M. B. Drysdale	JCB
		(17)	M.M. 22619 Sgt F.E. Handley; 50436 Pte T. Andrews; 102564 " A Peterson; 201014 L/c W Marshall; 265263 Pte Cragg A.H; 207923 " A Colledge; 126571 " A Ford; 106135 " A Demaine; 202115 Cpl F Mosby; 200926 Sgt L Garton; 74024 Pte T. Charnley; 200214 Sgt (A/CSM) P. Pearson (CSM); 20565 Pte W.R Whittaker; 57574 L/c Hardcastle, H.; 18575 Cpl H. Holmes; 13064 Pte D Macpherson; 202035 Cpl H Jebb	JCB
		(2)	Cards of Commendation G.O.C. 59th Division 67600 Pte F Bell; 67069 " J. V. Windle	

J.C. Baines Lt. Col
Commanding 2/5th Sher. Foresters

D. D. & L., London, E.C. (A8001) Wt. W1771/M2031 750,000 5/17 Sch. 52 Forms/C2118/14

Copy No. 6

2/8th. Battalion, The Sherwood Foresters ORDER No.[illegible]

W A R N I N G   O R D E R   No. 1
1.6.1918.

1. The Battalion, minus Transport, will proceede by BUS to PERNES, to-morrow.
The Transport will march to PERNES, via LISBOURG, where it will stay the night, June 2/3rd. (Billets from Sub-Area Commandant)

2. Billets will be given later.

3. ACKNOWLEDGE.

M O Barrows
Captain and Adjutant,
2/8th. Battalion, The Sherwood Foresters.

Issued at 7.45 p.m.

DISTRIBUTION.

Copy No, 1 Commanding Officer.
2 Headquarters,
3 R.S.M.
4 Quartermaster
5 Transport Corporal.
6 File.
7 & 8 War Diary.

Secret

No. 6

2/[illegible] Battalion, The Sherwood Foresters [illegible]

1. The Battalion will move in accordance with [illegible] issued to-day.

2. Parade [illegible] a.m. at Headquarters Mess. Dress - Full Marching Order, [illegible] Blankets to be carried.
All Officers' kits, Mess Boxes, Cooking Utensils, Rations and bicycles, will be dumped at Headquarters Mess at [illegible] a.m.
Mess Cart to be loaded by [illegible] a.m.
G.S. Wagon loaded ready with stores, Water Cart, and all Riding Horses will be ready to move off at Headquarters Mess at [illegible]
The following will proceed with Transport by road :-
Lieut. and Q.M. J. [illegible]
Corporal [illegible] Smith
A.S.C. Wagon Driver,
Mess Cart Driver
Water Cart Driver.
The four grooms who are not Officers Servants.
They will be ready to proceed with Transport at above time.

3. Breakfast [illegible] a.m.

4. Acknowledge.

M W Barrows
Captain and Adjutant,
2/[illegible] Battalion, The Sherwood Foresters.

Issued at [illegible] p.m.

DISTRIBUTION.

Copy No. 1 Headquarters.
[illegible] Quartermaster
[illegible] R.S.M.
[illegible] Corpl. Smith
[illegible] File
6 & 7 War Diary.

Copy no 6

SECRET. 2/5th. Battalion, The Sherwood Foresters ORDER No. 7

1. The Battalion will move tomorrow 7th, instant to HUMBERT, (about 8 miles)

2. Training Staff will parade ready to move off at 11 a.m. Dress Full marching order, Soft caps. Route ;- LA RUE NOIRE + BIMONT - ESCORTIER - HUMBERT. Captain J.N. Jacques and Lieut. A.H.G. Palmer will be with this party.

3, Transport will be ready to move off in square at 11 a.m. under Captain C.N. Littleboy (M.O.), via HUCQUELIERS - MANINGHEM - QUILEN.

4. Corpl. Shaw and Private Williams will remain behind with "Lorry Stores" to be fetched 8th. instant.

5. Instructions. All blankets, Officer s' Kits and stores for 1st. load to be at Battalion Headquarters Mess at 10.30 a.m. Rations for dinner to be cooked to- day and carried cold. Lieut. L.B. Lewis and the Interpreter on bicycles will proceed to HUMBERT to arrange billets. All Officers not detailed may proceed independently.

6, Acknowledge.

M D Barrows.
Captain and Adjutant,
2/5th. Battalion, The Sherwood Foresters.

Issued at 7.40 p.m.

Distribution.

Copy No.		
	1	Headquarters
	2	Quartermaster.
	3	R.S.M.
	4	Corpl. Shaw.
	5	File
	6 & 7	War Diary.

SECRET Copy No. 6

2/5th. Battalion, Sherwood Foresters ORDER No. [illegible]

Reference Map, CALAIS 13. 9.6.1918.

1. The Battalion will move to-morrow the 10th. instant, to RECLINGHEM (about 3 miles).

2. Parade at Starting Point - road junction in square PREURES - at 10.30 a.m. Dress Full Marching Order, soft caps. Route ENQUIN - RECLINGHEM.

3. The Intelligence Officer, the Interpreter and Corpl. Mosby will report to Headquarters, 47th. Infantry Brigade at PARENTY at 10 a.m., for billeting.

4. Instructions. Blankets, Stores and Officers(Kits to be outside Headquarters Mess at 10 a.m. G.S. Wagon and Mess Cart to report at Headquarters Mess at 10 a.m. Reveille and Breakfast as per Routine Orders. Dinners on arrival. Para. [illegible] of Routine Orders cancelled.

5. ACKNOWLEDGE.

M W Barrows
Captain and Adjutant,
2/5th. Battalion, The Sherwood Foresters.

Issued at 10 p.m.

Distribution.

Copy No.	
1	Headquarters
2	R.S.M.
3	Quartermaster
4	Corpl. Mosby
5	File
6 & 7	War Diary.

Army Form C. 2118.

Instructions regarding War Diaries and Intelligence Summaries are contained in F. S. Regs., Par. II. and the Staff Manual respectively. Title pages will be prepared in manuscript.

WAR DIARY

~~or~~

~~INTELLIGENCE SUMMARY.~~

(*Erase heading not required.*)

JR 18

Place	Date	Hour	Summary of Events and Information	Remarks and references to Appendices
	1918		2/5th Battalion, The Sherwood Foresters.	
	July			
BEZINGHEM.	1		The month of July was spent by the Training cadre	
			in Bezinghem, with no especial job. Ordinary training was	
			carried on with in the morning, and cricket, running,	
			and rifle meetings filled in the spare time. A certain	JBS
			amount of river bathing and walking took place, &	
	to		basket-ball & base-ball were also played. Many	
			rumours as to our disposal were in evidence during	
			the month. Of many cricket matches we played against	JBS
			neighbouring units, one only was lost.	
			The battalion was disbanded on 3rd August.	See op. Orders attached
			The Commanding Officer proceeded to COs pool, ETAPLES	
	Aug		& the Q.M. to Q.Ms pool, CALAIS, — the remainder	
	3		to 1/5th Sherwood Foresters	
			J.W. Burns [signature] Lt. Col.	
			Cdg 2/5 B'n The Sherwood Foresters	

A6945 Wt. W11422/M1160 35,000 12/16 D. D. & L. Forms/C.2118/14

SECRET. Copy No...4...

2/5th. Battalion, The Sherwood Foresters ORDER No. [illegible]

1. The Battalion will be disbanded on the 3rd. instant.

2. All personnel less Lieut.Colonel J.C. Baines D.S.O., Captain and Quartermaster J Farnsworth, and transport personnel as detailed below, willproceed to join the 1/5th. Battalion, The Sherwood Foresters by train, leaving SAMER, 8 p.m. under Captain R.S. Pratt M.C.
   Parade 5.30 p.m. Orderly Room Field.
   Dress Full Marching Order less packs, Soft Caps, Officers mounted.

3. The following will remain with transport and riding horses till no longer required, and will then proceed to join 1/5th. Sherwood Foresters.
   Corpl. Smith W.E.
   Pte. Bromfield
   Pte. Stone S
   Pte. Watts W.W. & Waugh
   Pte. Youngman S (to proceed to 7th. Suffolk Regt)

   Riding horses and transport will be handed in to 39th. Divisional train, c/o Area Commandant, SAMER under arrangements of Quartermaster.
   Riders will from there be sent to LOSTRAT, and disposed of to Field Remount Section, Army Artillery Section, TILQUES.
   Transport will be sent to A.H.T.D. CUCQ, ETAPLES.

4. Officers' Kits, O.R. Stores, and packs of Staff to be dumped at Officers' Mess by 4 p.m.

5. Acknowledge.

Issued at 3.20 p.m. 2.2.1918.

DISTRIBUTION.

Copy No.	
1	Quartermaster
2	R.S.M.
3	File
4 & 5	War Diary.

Captain and Adjutant,
2/5th. Battalion, The Sherwood Fors.

www.ingramcontent.com/pod-product-compliance
Lightning Source LLC
Chambersburg PA
CBHW080854230426
43662CB00013B/2101